INNER VOICES

A GUIDE FOR FREEING YOUR MIND

CHANA MASON

Praise for Chana Mason's Work

I'm so grateful that I found Chana Mason and her e-course. I have been doing The Work of Byron Katie consistently for a year and had made a lot of progress, but found myself stuck on some of my biggest problematic thoughts. Chana has developed incredibly helpful tools and showed us the practical, step-by-step application of each. She worked with us on an individual basis as well as a group. These tools have made all the difference for me. Doing this course was one of the best decisions of the year.

—Carol Johnson, USA

One session and I got it! Chana understood and simplified my thoughts, she helped me understand where my thoughts were coming from and showed me how to stop and change the path of thinking. And it was also un a fun way!

—Karen Sevilla, Mexico

I love my sessions with Chana. She really helps me unpack those old beliefs and seriously turn them around. I'm always excited knowing that the days after the session will be characterized by deep paradigm shifts!

—Daniella Goldfine, Israel

Chana is a no BS coach. She gets right to the core of the issue and handles it with grace and compassion. She's empathetic but also an amazing accountability partner. I highly recommend Chana to anyone who wants to take their life and their strengths to the next level!

—Rachel Gluck, Israel

These classes have changed my life. It's amazing how just learning about where the work really is, the blaming and fighting almost immediately stops. Personally, my relationships got healthier and happier from just that first small step. And that includes the relationship with myself and my relationship with Gd ;) what hit me the strongest were the turnarounds and realizing these thoughts are here for me.

—Leah Mistrel, Israel

As a Wellness professional reading Hold That Thought and leading a group through the worksheets and chapters, I can say this book had a truly amazing effect. These easy to grasp introspective techniques are not only SUPER beneficial tools for any person, but they are also really easy to understand. All of our book group thoroughly enjoyed this, and I am still talking with them about how they're implementing these techniques on a regular basis. I will definitely be using the material from this book for many years to come.

—Alyson O, USA

We together broke down my thought patterns and belief systems. I started to create the beliefs that I want in my life ... how I see things, how I view others and myself. I've gotten more control over my thinking and over my life in general!

—Naomi Klein, Israel

Thank you for the life coaching sessions!! I'm living my dream life. I can tell every day that I have been strengthened and found a connection to some deep love from working with you!

—Evelyn Masoner, USA

Since coming into my orbit Chana has helped me find new perspectives and made my star shine brighter.

—Rebekah Saltzman, Host of Balagan Be Gone Podcast

Chana helped me break through challenges I deemed insurmountable and too painful. In a matter of a few sessions, I made progress that felt should have taken years. My meetings with Chana not only helped me overcome distress and difficulty, they improved my wellbeing and inner peace.

—G.M., Israel

I was really struggling when I first started working with Chana. By the time we finished our coaching, my business had completely turned itself around. Chana is truly gifted at guiding a person to bring their best self and to realize their goals and dreams. Being coached by Chana was one of the best things I've ever done for myself. It was a life-changing experience, and I highly recommend her as a coach for anyone who is struggling to achieve their dreams.

—Amanda Luzzader, USA

I am a licensed clinical social worker and I have implemented the strategies I learned into my own life and my private practice! I have been blown away when I guide a client through their stressful thought and how clearly they can see that it is only a thought that does not have power over them. By the time we are done the session, clients are shocked they are looking at things differently and they feel so relieved and free. Personally, I feel so much more at peace. I find myself talking myself through challenging thoughts and situations. have used the strategies with my husband, my children, and my mother. It has really been life-changing. The book was simple and easy to read. The course was very useful and helped me to see the process.

—Jessica Bibeau, USA

Cover Design by Shefa Rumby
Layout by Zoran Maksimović
and Md Mosarof Hossain
Cartoons by Eduardo Comoglio

Learn more at ChanaMason.com/Inner-Voices

I dedicate this book to my Papi, Alberto Gateño.
Even before I was born, you've loved me
from the deepest depths of your heart.
But I didn't always know it.
Thank you for being patient enough for me to come around.

Table of Contents

Introduction

Our experience of life comes from the inside out.

If I expect all Arabs to be terrorists; then every time I pass one here in Jerusalem, I'll watch out for danger signals, question their behavior, and keep my distance. The result? My body will tense up, my heart will race, my breathing will stop. I'll terrorize *myself* with my belief.

You may wish to argue that, living in Jerusalem, I have reasons to be suspicious. In the two decades I've lived here, there've been dozens of terrorist attacks in my neighborhood, local shops, buses, etc. That's all true. What is also true is that in all that time, I've shared a city with thousands of Arabs, and not once did any of them lay a hand on me. And even if one had, that would be one moment out of hundreds of thousands I've experienced here.

Also true is that in countless moments, Arabs have greeted me kindly, engaged in positive business dealings with me, offered me assistance, or simply ignored me and went on their merry way.

So which story do I live? The one where all these people are out to kill me, or the one where we're all just doing the best we can to live our lives peacefully? It comes down to what *I choose to focus on.*

More importantly, it comes down to how I want to *feel* on a daily basis. Do I want to feel constantly terrorized or constantly supported? In stress or at peace?

If you're new to everything I'm saying here and don't believe your emotional experience is a choice, then Inquiry may be the kindest gift you can give yourself.

Inquiry is the ability to question your thinking, assumptions, and beliefs. It has transformed my life from one of anxiety to one of ever-blossoming joy and peace. Inquiry is at the center of my coaching practice, as it quickly helps people gain clarity and experience calm.

Over the years, other coaches and therapists have asked me for advice on how to facilitate their clients through Inquiry, which led me to write *Hold That Thought*. I've gotten requests from readers, who loved the clarity of ideas and tools in the book, asking for specific strategies and guidelines for facilitating *themselves* with a journal.

This book is divided into three sections. In Hearing the Voice, you'll learn tools for identifying the thoughts blocking your peace and joy. In Feeling the Voice, you'll learn how to tune into the signals your body's giving you. In Strengthening the Voice, you'll learn how to shift your beliefs so you can live in alignment with your values and desires.

You'll learn a new tool in each chapter of *Inner Voices* through dialogues I've had with actual clients or my own journal entries. Names and identifying characteristics of the clients have been altered to protect their privacy. Any resemblance to someone you actually know (including yourself) is only a reflection of the universality of our struggles.

So, here we are, on a journey of understanding, questioning, and shifting our thoughts. I hope this journey guides you towards more compassion, insight, and unbridled happiness!

If you have benefited from any of the teachings shared in this book, or if you have tools or insights of your own, I would love to hear from you.

Wishing you many little joys!
Chana Mason
Jerusalem, Israel

Visit my site at **ChanaMason.com**
Email me at **Chana@ChanaMason.com**

Inquiry 101

By doubting we are led to question,
by questioning we arrive at the truth.

—Peter Abelard

B yron Katie says, "An unquestioned mind is the world of suffering." Why? Has anyone ever said you were too stupid, too short, too slow, or too careless? More importantly, did you believe them? If you haven't questioned their words, you're likely suffering.

It's only because people questioned the presumption that humans couldn't fly, that we can traverse the world in mere hours. Because he questioned the limitation of a four-minute mile, Roger Bannister opened the gates for thousands of runners to beat that record after him.

And it's due to your willingness to question the stuck-ness of your situation— the presumed traps of your upbringing, social status, or circumstances—that you've reached for this book. You instinctively know you're able to change your mind and thus change your *life*.

Shifting your mindset begins with a keen awareness of the beliefs upsetting you, questioning those thoughts, and replacing them with thoughts which bring you joy and peace.

I've dedicated countless years to learning tools to free my mind. Along the way, I've created new tools to help my clients gain clarity and experience breakthroughs. I've developed new paradigms to help the thousands of students I teach around the world. You'll learn these tools and paradigms in my books, and if you apply them, you'll expand your consciousness into higher states of calm, clarity, and joy.

First, though, I want to make sure you learn (and ideally memorize) the core tool I teach my clients, students, and readers. *The Work of Byron Katie* is the simplest tool for Inquiry I've ever encountered. Everything I teach in this book expounds on it. In each chapter of this book, I'll share a tool and how I use it in my journal or in a dialogue with a client. The dialogues include other forms of Inquiry that I pull from *The Journey* of Brandon Bays, *The Option Process* of Barry Neil Kaufman, Neuro-Linguistic Programming, and those of my own design.

When you're facilitating yourself, though, I recommend you keep it simple. Stick with *The Work* and add tools one at a time as you integrate them.

So, what's *The Work?*

First, identify a thought that upsets you. (You'll be learning lots of tools for doing this in the coming chapters.)

For example, this morning I woke up with a migraine. And the first thought that came into my mind was, "Today is going to be horrible."

This thought is clearly a downer; it crushes my desire to get out of bed, meet the day, simply live. Because I didn't want to continue feeling that way, I did Inquiry using The Work of Byron Katie.

I asked myself the following four questions. There are no "right" answers, just honest ones.

1. Is it true? (This is a question straight to your gut.)

    Yes!

2. Can I absolutely know it's true?

    No.

3. How do I react when I believe that thought? (Emotions, physical sensations, behaviors)

    All the energy drains out of me. I feel sad. My chest gets tight. I imagine a horrible-looking day and don't want to get out of bed. I crave chocolate and movies.

4. How am I without the thought? (Take a deep breath and imagine yourself in the situation without the thought — if you need help on this one, refer to "The Little Green Troll" chapter in *Hold That Thought.*)

I just want to get up and brush my teeth. I can think about the next step in front of me and focus on how I want to spend my day.

The last step in *The Work* is where all the magic happens. It helps you learn from upsetting beliefs so you can use them to fuel your life forward. Simply write the opposite of the original thought by saying the opposite of ONE WORD from the statement. Katie calls these new perspectives "turnarounds."

So, *today is going to be horrible* can become:

Today is not going to be horrible.

Today is going to be fantastic.

Today is going to be what it's going to be.

Each turnaround offers your mind a new way of seeing so it's not stuck in a pattern of misery. Each new perspective literally expands your consciousness and frees you to choose beliefs that bring you joy. So your mind can take them seriously, offer evidence for why they're true. Just like a chair needs at least three legs to stand, so do your turnarounds.

Let's look at the first turnaround. *Today is not going to be horrible.* What reasons can I think of to support this thought?

1.   My body is intact.

2.   I'm going to have lunch with great friends.

3.   I have a book I'm excited to write.

I'm actually typing these words with the same headache. And though it hurts, I could still go grocery shopping, make breakfast, and sit down at my computer. Not so horrible, eh?

We then engage in the same process for the other turnarounds.

Today is going to be fantastic.

1.   I have food to eat.

2.   I have electricity and running water.

3.   I don't have to work today unless I want to.

4.   The temperature is awesome, and the sky is a gorgeous blue.

Today is going to be what it's going to be.

1.   Time is going to pass, and the day is going to happen with or without my judgement of it.

2. I can choose to observe it or fight it. I'd be more peaceful just riding the day like a wave.

3. My calling it "horrible" doesn't make it better; it just makes me lethargic and upset.

To review, *The Work* involves four questions and the turnarounds:

1. **Is it true?** (This is a question straight to your gut.)

2. **Can I absolutely know it's true?**

3. **How do I react when I believe that thought?** (Emotions, physical sensations, behaviors)

4. **How am I without the thought?**

    Turn it around: What's the opposite of the belief? Offer at least 3 reasons this new perspective is as true or more true than the original statement.

In the coming chapters, you'll learn how to use Inquiry in your daily life, facilitating yourself just like I facilitate my clients. I'll show you how I do Journal Inquiry using nothing more than paper and pen (though I recommend you buy an attractive journal and a special pen to make the experience more delicious.)

I look forward to sharing this journey with you!

See an **Inquiry** in action and
get **Free Bonus Materials** for *Inner Voices* at:

ChanaMason.com/Inner-Voices-Bonus.

HEARING THE VOICE

*A man is but the product of his thoughts.
What he thinks, he becomes.*

—Mahatma Gandhi

The One Question

Try not to listen to all the voices in your head.
But listen to the one voice that really matters.
The one that is telling you to stay calm.

—Avijeet Das

Melissa always wanted to travel and explore a new language and culture but had never left the comfort of the United States. Year after year, she'd gab to her girlfriends about the hikes she'd love to take, the foods she'd taste, and the people she'd meet. So her friends gathered the money together to buy her a plane ticket to Italy for her 50th birthday.

Sounds great, right?

Melissa contacted me in a panic. "S.O.S! I need a session ASAP!"

She was having panic attacks just thinking about the flight reservation, much less the trip itself.

Panic attacks are a physiological experience, and just like any other emotion or sensation, they're the product of thoughts we're harboring in our mind. One way to shift our emotional experience is to shift our thinking. But first, we need to know what we're believing.

"Let's ask The One Question," I told Melissa, "do you remember it?"

"What am I believing that's making me feel this way?"

From Melissa's answer to The One Question, we're able to build a Thought Bank, a collection of beliefs she has about this topic. We'll use the Thought Bank as the basis of our work together.

Chana: So what are you believing at the moment you see the flight reservation that makes you anxious?

Melissa: Something bad is going to happen. I won't be able to take care of myself. I won't be safe. I won't be able to go home if I need to.

Chana: Anything else?

Melissa: If I don't feel well, I won't be able to go back to my hotel. It's too far from home.

Melissa's Thought Bank

Something bad is going to happen.

I won't be able to take care of myself.

I won't be safe.

I will need to go home.

I won't be able to go home.

I won't feel well.

If I don't feel well, I won't be able to go back to my hotel.

It's too far from home.

It's too scary.

I can't handle a trip like this.

I can't handle being far from home.

Chana: Is that all?

Melissa: I won't be safe. It's too scary. That's what keeps running through my mind: that I won't be safe.

As Melissa spoke, I wrote the Thought Bank into my notebook. You can do this for yourself when you're working on your own. This is what I wrote:

Note that some of what I've included doesn't exactly match what Melissa stated outright. As an outsider, I have the advantage of hearing what she's implying between the lines. That doesn't always mean my guesses are correct, so I have to check if my collection matches her actual beliefs.

Chana: Does this list resonate with you?

Melissa: Yes. Especially what you said at the end. I feel silly believing this. I'm a mother of grown children. I've run a successful business. I should be able to travel just like everyone else, but really, I don't believe I can handle it.

Chana: Let's add what you just said to our Thought Bank. "You should be able to travel just like everyone else."

Melissa: Yeah. I feel so dumb.

Chana: Why?

Melissa: Because I've talked forever about going on an adventure. And my friends worked so hard to surprise me with this trip. But really, I'm too scared to go.

Chana: Why?

Melissa: I just keep coming back to not being safe.

Chana: So let's look at that belief. Picture yourself looking at that flight reservation. You won't be safe, is it true?

Melissa: Yes!

Chana: Can you absolutely know it's true?

Melissa: Yes. I mean, there are muggers and criminals in every country, especially a mafia-ridden country like Italy. I don't speak the language. I won't know what to do or where to go…

Chana: And how do you react when you believe you won't be safe?

Melissa: I get panicky. I feel like I can't breathe.

Chana: How do you behave when you believe it?

Melissa: I just want to hide. I don't want to talk to anyone or look at anything. I just want to go home and crawl into bed.

Chana: Not so adventurous, huh?

Melissa: Not at all.

Chana: Take a deep breath and imagine yourself looking at the flight reservation again. Picture the thought "you won't be safe" stepping away from you and escaping out the window. How are you without it?

Melissa: Calmer. My chest isn't so tight.

Melissa saw how this thought affected her and how she'd be without it. By exploring alternative ways of thinking, she was free to ingrain new neural connections to replace patterns that made her suffer. Byron Katie calls these alternatives *turnarounds*, which are opposites of the original thought. Turnarounds offer insights into how we can live with joy and in alignment with our values. To help these new beliefs take root, we need to fertilize them with evidence.

Chana: Let's shift our thinking a bit. Give me one opposite of the statement "you won't be safe."

Melissa: I will be safe.

Chana: Give me three reasons why that's true.

Melissa: My friends picked Italy because it's a pretty safe country. They're not interested in sending me to the wolves. (Laughs.)

Chana: Why'd you laugh?

Melissa: Because I was actually picturing getting off the plane and being ravaged by greasy Italian men as if they were a pack of werewolves. My imagination was coming up with the craziest stuff.

Chana: It had to. Your mind is a fabulous servant. If you believe you won't be safe, it has to give you evidence proving you right, even if it has to fantasize that evidence.

Melissa: I think I have to give my mind better orders.

Chana: Exactly. You can do that by training it to seek evidence for beliefs that bring you peace. So give me another reason it's true that you *will* be safe.

Melissa: I'll be traveling with a friend and we're both pretty street smart.

Chana: And all this time I thought you'd be traveling alone.

Melissa: I guess I failed to share that detail.

Chana: Sure. It made your situation seem more dire. But now that you're choosing calm, give me another reason you'll be safe.

Melissa: I know how to call for help if I need it. I don't speak Italian, but most people speak enough English to understand a woman screaming HELP!

Chana: Give me one more reason.

Melissa: I might get pick-pocketed, but I've never heard of tourists in Italy getting stabbed or murdered or anything. I won't like losing money if that happens, but I wouldn't be in physical danger.

Chana: Let's explore another turnaround. What's another opposite of "you won't be safe?"

Melissa: I won't be unsafe.

Chana: How's that true?

Melissa: There are doctors and hospitals there if I get sick.

Chana: What else?

Melissa: There's modern plumbing, so I can assume there won't be cholera.

Chana: And...

Melissa: And Lisa and I will look out for each other. We're too old to be out late at night, so we'll usually be roaming the streets when they're still bustling with people.

Chana: What's another turnaround?

Melissa: Um.... I can't think of one.

Chana: When you've got a statement that begins with "I," you can replace it with "my thoughts." So "I won't be safe" becomes...

Melissa: ... my thoughts won't be safe?

Chana: Exactly. Your mind has been feeding you beliefs that scare you. But you can put it in its place. Ideally, you want it to be your servant and not your master. You want it to feed you thoughts that lead you where you want to go.

Melissa: And not into total panic. But when I'm believing that I won't be safe, I already feel tight. I don't feel safe right now.

Chana: Right. You're safe all along, but…

Melissa: My thoughts won't be safe if it keeps going in this direction, rerunning all this garbage that's in my Thought Bank.

Chana: How do you feel?

Melissa: Lighter. I knew my thoughts were causing my anxiety, but I thought of them as MY thoughts. But if they were really *mine*, I'd pick totally different thoughts. They're *totally* not mine. They're foreign invaders.

Chana: So what do you want to do?

Melissa: I want to believe that I will be safe, that I won't be unsafe.

Chana: And how can you take action to further ingrain those new beliefs in your mind?

Melissa: I can talk to friends who've been to Italy and ask them about their experiences.

Chana: What else?

Melissa: I can think about my many visits to Philly or New York, where even though there's no lack of crime, I've always been safe.

Chana: You can play those memories in your mind and say to yourself, "I'm safe. I will be safe."

Melissa: Like a mantra?

Chana: Yes. You can also just look for evidence in your everyday life. Like every time you turn on the heat, you can notice how safe you are from the elements. Or when you flush the toilet, how it's keeping you safe from disease.

Melissa: And every time I do that, I can say, "I'm safe." That's easy enough.

Chana: Anything else you can do?

Melissa: I can learn a little Italian, especially words that make me feel safer, like about getting food, help, or a bathroom. There's still something nagging at me, though.

Chana: What's that?

Melissa: That it *feels* safer to be close to home.

Chana: We can explore that. Does being in the U.S. make you safer?

Melissa: It feels like it.

Chana: Sometimes it helps to define your terms. What do you mean when you say "safe?"

Melissa: Hmm. Good question. Well… Being safe means not being in physical danger.

Chana: What kind of danger?

Melissa: Like getting stabbed. Or raped. Or getting hurt.

Chana: Does being close to home prevent those things?

Melissa: I want to say yes.

Chana: That's the emotional part of you. Inquiry demands we use our logical faculties. So ask yourself, are people who get stabbed or raped or hurt usually far from home?

Melissa: Hmmm… probably not. They're probably in their own city. Especially with rape. I remember hearing perpetrators are usually someone the victim knows personally.

Chana: So does being close to home make you safer?

Melissa: It means I know my way around and where to go. Like in Philly; I know what parts of town to avoid.

Chana: How do you know that?

Melissa: I guess people told me. And some places you can just tell from the graffiti or the garbage on the streets or the people just hanging around on street corners.

Chana: Did you always know that about Philly?

Melissa: No. We live an hour away. The first time I went there, I didn't know my way around at all.

Chana: Just like in Italy.

Melissa: Oh! …. That's true. I could do the same thing I did in Philly. I could ask people. I could look for signs that an area isn't safe. And it's not like when I was a teenager going into the city for the first time. Now I have GPS, and there are travel books and blogs and virtual tour guides, and real tour guides.

Chana: How do you feel?

Melissa: Excited! I just realized how many resources there are. Just GPS alone keeps me from getting lost. That's a pretty safe tool. And you know what?

Chana: What?

Melissa: I have a bunch of friends whose parents or grandparents came here from Italy. They are the loudest, friendliest people I know. I bet I'll meet Italians who would be happy to help me if I need it.

Chana: Especially the men, *bella.*

Melissa: (Laughs) Now that's true!

Melissa panicked at the thought of travel, even though it was always her dream. Asking The One Question gave her access to the beliefs causing her anxiety.

The One Question is the *most important* lesson in this book. I recommend you memorize it because it can be life-altering.

What am I believing right now that's making me feel this way?

Embedded in this little question are so many big ideas:

1. Beliefs, and not my circumstances, are causing my feelings.

2. I can identify those beliefs simply by asking for them.

3. These beliefs are separate from me; they don't define me.

4. By putting them down on paper, I can separate myself from them.

5. I can do something with these beliefs to change my feelings.

Questioning her beliefs around safety helped Melissa see how many resources were available, both inside of herself and from the world around her, all conspiring to keep her alive, healthy, and safe. This doesn't guarantee that nothing bad will ever happen to her, but exploring turnarounds helped Melissa see that, under most circumstances and at most times, she's actually safe.

TUNING IN

Now it's your turn to practice asking The One Question. In your journal, dedicate a fresh page to a new Thought Bank you're about to create. Think of a specific moment in time (that you can clearly picture) when you felt upset. Ask yourself the question:

What am I believing right now that's making me feel this way?
Or
What was I believing then that made me feel that way?

At the top of your journal page, write: My Thought Bank about…. (e.g. My neighbor, the upcoming elections, yesterday's class.)

Then write every thought that comes up in response to The One Question. Putting the thoughts to paper can already distance you from them. You can now observe them, question them, and choose a different way of thinking. In the next chapter, I'll give you a peek into my journal and show you how I used Journaling Inquiry to relieve my anxiety about wasting time.

Journaling Inquiry

Whether you're keeping a journal or writing as a meditation, it's the same thing. What's important is you're having a relationship with your mind.

—Natalie Goldberg

A year and a half into the global Covid-19 saga, my body was wound up like a spring in a jack-in-the-box. My heart was constantly aflutter. I was checking the news and stats multiple times a day, and I couldn't imagine meditating, much less sitting still. I wanted to use my time productively, but kept binging on books or videos. Something had to change, or I was going to pop.

So, I booked myself a small B&B in the desert by the Dead Sea. No phone. No books. No computer. No people.

Just me, a suitcase full of mangoes, and the quiet of the desert.

Turns out, I didn't need all those stimuli, because my mind was racing so fast, it gave me enough distractions, stories, memories, songs, regrets, and fears to fuel Hollywood for the next century.

It kept nagging me that I wasn't *getting anything done.* I wasn't writing books or seeing clients or running workshops. And to top it all off, I only did one thing at a time. I set a rule that I was EITHER cutting a mango OR eating a mango OR painting OR doing yoga OR hiking OR meditating. NO multitasking.

The whole excursion was a horror movie: *Nightmare of the Unproductive.*

If I didn't shift my mindset, my sweet desert excursion would be ruined. So, I popped open my journal and began an Inquiry, a process of pinpointing the beliefs distressing me, questioning them, and shifting my mindset.

I asked myself The One Question, "What am I believing that's making me feel I'm in a nightmare?"

I asked myself The One Question, "What am I believing that's making me feel I'm in a nightmare?"

I wrote my responses in my journal:

I'm not getting anything done. This is a waste of my time. I should be more productive. I should be making money right now. I should be working. I know I feel calmer when I do one thing at a time, but I'm wasting time when I'm not doing two or three productive things at once, like watching a nutrition video while I do yoga, or chatting with my mom on the phone while I shop for groceries.

The thought bothering me most was, if I'm not multitasking, I'm wasting time.

So, I wrote that statement on the top of a new journal page and engaged in Journal Inquiry. Because it's the simplest tool for Inquiry, I used *The Work* of Byron Katie.

I've found it helpful to review this process repeatedly until it's memorized. So, to review, I first ask myself the following four questions. There are no "right" answers, just honest ones.

1. **Is it true?** (This is a question straight to your gut.)

2. **Can I absolutely know that it's true?**

3. **How do I react when I believe that thought?** (List emotions, physical sensations, behaviors.)

4. **How am I without the thought?** (Take a deep breath and imagine yourself in the situation without the thought.)

Because I'm so familiar with *The Work*, I prefer to use notation in my journal, rather than writing out each question. You'll see my short form and then Katie's original questions in parentheses for reference.

If I'm not multitasking, I'm wasting time.

True? (Is it true?)

Yes!

Absolutely? (Can I absolutely Know that it's true?)

No.

React? (How do I react when I believe that thought?)
Breathing tightens. Antsy, look to fill time, even with
dumb stuff. I lose track of things, feel fretful and
frustrated. I don't stop and plan, so I keep walking
around in circles.

Without? (How am I without that thought?)

I feel ease, open breathing, space to think.

Once I felt the agonizing pain of believing *and* the delicious pleasure of not believing the thought, I was itching for an alternative. This meant I was ready for turnarounds, opposites of the original statement. I did this by flipping ONE WORD, which created an entirely new belief. Because I wanted my mind to take this new perspective seriously, I needed to offer at least three pieces of evidence proving it true. I made sure to give more than three reasons to support my turnarounds because I was particularly attached to the original thought and wanted to bolster alternatives.

@ (turnaround) -> If I'm multitasking, I'm wasting time
(What reasons can I offer for why this new belief is
as true or truer than the original?)

1. I can't be present, which is the only time I really have.

2. I miss out on greeting people who are in front of
   me when I'm on the phone running errands

3. I'm more likely to burn dinner

4. I don't meditate and breathe during yoga, which is
   half the point

31

5. I fill my head with a lot of noise, which creates clutter and makes it hard to think clearly the rest of the day.

6. No deep work, which is where I experience deep satisfaction

@ If I'm not multitasking, I'm basking in time

1. I feel calmer, enjoy more

2. Life is richer

3. I'm less agitated, hurried

4. I can be more present for my clients

5. I'm disconnected from my phone, which pulls me into another space/time

These new perspectives offered a slew of insights, but if not taken into action, they are unlikely to create genuine change. So the next question I asked myself is, "How can I actualize these turnarounds in my life?"

In this situation, I created rules and wrote them down in my journal:

Times I'm okay with multitasking:
1. Doing dishes
2. Housekeeping
3. Folding Laundry

Times music is enriching:
1. Yoga
2. Cooking

3. Dancing
4. Doing art

Have I kept to my rules perfectly? No, to be honest. But they have informed my day-to-day since the retreat. I'm more likely to leave my phone at home when I go out on walks, to cook with music rather than videos, and to carve time for daily meditation, yoga, or contemplation. After four days of desert-infused quiet, my nervous system unwound, and I've been able to carry the quiet with me by focusing more on presence than on multitasking.

In the coming chapters, I'll be introducing tools through dialogues I've had with clients because I find them to be more dynamic, interesting, and informative than me yapping about myself for pages on end. When you practice applying the tools, though, I recommend you keep coming back to the journal format I shared above as the central anchor of your work.

TUNING IN

Now it's your turn to practice Journaling Inquiry. In your journal, write one belief from the Thought Bank you gathered in response to The One Question. Ask yourself Katie's four questions. Turn that thought around and see what you can learn from the new perspectives. Then consider how you can take action on the turnarounds and act as soon as you can!

The Rant

> *"Sometimes at night I lie awake*
> *and quarrel with the voices in my head.*
>
> —*Pat Barker"*

R uby's heart was thumping so loudly, even I could sense it. Her energy was scattered, her movements were erratic, and words tumbled out of her mouth.

"I just can't handle it," she cried as she plopped herself onto the couch, "it's too much!"

"What's too much?" I asked.

"Everything! It's so overwhelming." Tears streamed down her face. "I don't even know what. But it's all too much."

Have you ever felt more emotions than you could easily handle, yet not know why? It's emotional chaos. You can bring order to the chaos by Ranting your story out, either to a coach or into your journal. (I first introduced The Rant in my book, *Hold That Thought.*)

"Let's start from the beginning. When did you start feeling this way?"

"Yesterday." Ruby's eyes welled up. "My ex-boyfriend, Johnny, showed up at my door. He said he wanted to talk. And I didn't want to talk…" She threw her hands up in the air. "But then he begged, and then I said okay, and then he ended up hanging out in my apartment for hours, and it became a tangled mess. He said he wanted to get back together. How am I supposed to respond to that? How could a girl not be flattered by that? Oh, yeah, and did I mention the flowers? I couldn't just push him away. He brought flowers!" Ruby grabbed a tissue and blew her nose. "And I want to get back together too, but…"

"But what?"

"But he wants to live on a farm and raise sheep for wool. I want to live in a city and work in high tech. Our lives are totally different, and that's not changing. I honestly can't stand the smell of sheep. There's no way I could live next to them. Ugh. But when he looks at me like that, how am I not supposed to melt?" She threw her arms up. "This is so complicated. I hate that it's so complicated. He should just be happy living in the city and having a dog or something. I could have a dog. But no. He won't let go of his stupid rancher dream and yet looks at me with those eyes. It's just so unfair!" Ruby blew her nose, shaking her head into the tissue.

"What is?"

"Love should be easy. If you meet someone, and they're meant to be, then it should be easy, shouldn't it? Whatever happened to 'all you need is love?' This would be so much easier if he just ran off with some other girl. Or if it turned out he was gay. Or if he had lots of acne. Then it wouldn't hurt so much."

"So what you want is to not hurt?" I asked.

"Yeah, duh. Isn't that obvious?"

"What's obvious to one person might not be obvious to another. I am simply seeking clarity. If you don't want to hurt, what do you want?"

Ruby's face grew pensive. Her eyes searched the room. "I want to be happy. I don't want to be crying all the time. I just want to be calm and happy and chill. And I want to think straight. Right now, I'm such a mess. I can't get any work done, and I can barely sleep."

"So, just to clarify: you want to be happy, calm, and chill. Correct?"

"Yeah."

"Great. Now we'll look at everything you've said, identify every belief you've stated overtly or implied, and question whether those beliefs are bringing you the happiness you seek."

When I'm on my own, I simply open my journal and scribble down my Rant. Had Ruby been working with a journal, her entry could have looked like this:

MY RANT

My ex-boyfriend, Johnny, showed up at my door. He said he wanted to talk. I didn't want to talk. But then he begged, and then I said okay, and then he ended up hanging out in my apartment for hours, and it became a tangled mess. He said he wanted to get back together.

How am I supposed to respond to that? How could a girl not be flattered by that? Oh, yeah, and did I mention the flowers? I couldn't just push him away. He brought flowers! And I want to get back together too, but he wants to live on a farm and raise sheep for wool. I want to live in a city and work in high tech. Our lives are totally different and that's not changing. I honestly can't stand the smell of sheep. There's no way I could live next to them. Ugh. But when he looks at me like that, how am I not supposed to melt? This is so complicated. I hate that it's so complicated. He should just be happy living in the city and having a dog or something. I could have a dog. But no, he won't let go of his stupid rancher dream and yet looks at me with those eyes. It's just so unfair! Love should be easy. If you meet someone, and they're meant to be, then it should be easy to know. Whatever happened to "all you need is love?" This would be so much easier if he just ran off with some other girl. Or if it turned out he was gay. Or if he had lots of acne. Then it wouldn't hurt so much.

WHAT I WANT

I want to be happy. I don't want to be crying all the time and just want to be calm and happy and chill. And I want to think straight. Right now I'm such a mess, I can't get any work done and I can barely sleep.

Ranting helps us get "everything out there" because it takes the chaos out of our minds and puts it onto paper. What it doesn't do is bring order and calm to the chaos. That's where Inquiry comes in. First, though, we need to identify exactly what beliefs we're harboring.

Let's walk through Ruby's Rant line-by-line.

My ex-boyfriend, Johnny, showed up at my door. He said he wanted to talk.

It's important to separate simple facts on the ground from beliefs. If a video camera could verify the contents of a statement, then it's a fact. Ruby's ex-boyfriend's presence at her door and request to talk could have been captured on film. Thus it's a fact. We don't add that to her Thought Bank because it doesn't need to be questioned.

I didn't want to talk. But then he begged, and then I said okay…

Ruby says she didn't want to talk, but we quickly see that she's talking to Johnny. Her words and actions are in contradiction, so I put her "not wanting to talk" into question and add it to the Thought Bank. The definition of "begging" is also a matter of opinion, so I'm adding it to my list.

In the charts below, you'll see sections of Ruby's Rant and the list of thoughts I assume she's believing about her situation. At times, I'm taking her words verbatim; at others, I'm taking guesses. You'll see that I've sometimes changed Ruby's words into clear sentences ripe for Inquiry. I look for statements that are causing her upset rather than the peace she's seeking. It'll be up to Ruby to correct me if my assumptions are off.

Inquiry is dependent on asking questions. We can question a statement, but we can't question a question. Try it and you'll see how confusing it can be. Below you'll see that I took Ruby's questions and turned them into statements.

Ruby's Rant	Thought Bank
My ex-boyfriend showed up at my door. He said he wanted to talk. And I didn't want to talk.	I didn't want to talk. He begged

My mind also questions whether Johnny "ended up" in her apartment as if he and Ruby are passive participants in their own lives.

Ruby's Rant	Thought Bank
… and then he ended up hanging out in my apartment for hours…	He ended up hanging out in my apartment for hours.
	I didn't want him in my apartment for hours.

When I read, "it became a tangled mess," I immediately want to ask, "what did?" I listed my attempts at an answer.

Ruby's Rant	Thought Bank
… and it became a tangled mess.	It became a tangled mess.
	I'm a tangled mess.
	We're a tangled mess.
	Our relationship is a tangled mess.
	I'm confused.
	I don't know what I want.

Sometimes we *say* we want one thing, but there's something else we're prioritizing. I question whether Johnny wants to get back together with Ruby or with a fantasy farmer girl he's projecting onto Ruby. If their values haven't changed, then his declaration that he "wants to get back together" is worth questioning.

Ruby's Rant	Thought Bank
He said he wanted to get back together. How am I supposed to respond to that?	He wanted to get back together with me.
	I didn't know how to respond.
	There's only one way for a girl to respond.

Rather than checking in with herself, Ruby is trying to project herself into the "norm." She questions whether she's responding the way other women would, rather than doing what's best for her.

Ruby's Rant	Thought Bank
How could a girl not be flattered by that?	A girl should be flattered by a boy's advancements.
	If I'm flattered, I can't think clearly.
	If someone wants me, I can't think about what I want.
	If someone wants me, what I want doesn't matter.

Johnny's flowers add an interesting twist to the situation. He's done something gracious, which, according to Ruby's rules, means she has to be gracious in return. We want to be liked by those around us and will often compromise ourselves, our values, or our dreams to be deemed nice, good, or successful. External praise is like candy. It offers a short-term high but doesn't nourish us in the long run.

Ruby's Rant	Thought Bank
Oh, yeah, and did I mention the flowers?! I couldn't just push him away. He brought flowers!	Being honest means I'm pushing him away.
	It's more important that Johnny think I'm nice than that I be honest with myself/him.
	I couldn't push him away.
	I couldn't push him away because he brought me flowers.
	If I pushed him away when he brought me flowers, I'd be mean/rude/unappreciative.

In the statements below, Ruby contradicts herself. She, too, wants to "get back together" with a fantasy.

Ruby's Rant	Thought Bank
And I want to get back together too, but he wants to live on a farm and raise sheep for wool. I want to live in a city and work in high tech. Our lives are totally different and that's not changing. I honestly can't stand the smell of sheep. There's no way I could live next to them. Ugh.	I want to get back together.

Ruby's asking me how she should feel and behave, rather than asking herself. She's presuming she's the object of another person's desires rather than an active participant in her own life. She doesn't have to take responsibility for what happens, which seems easy until she has to face the consequences of acting against her values.

Here it seems innocent, but if hard drugs, alcohol, or sex were involved, she'd put herself in danger with this logic. That's how people say that a sexual encounter "just happened," when, in reality, two engaged adults have to take many conscious actions to make such an encounter possible.

Ruby's Rant	Thought Bank
But when he looks at me like that, how am I not supposed to melt?	I have to melt when he looks at me like that.
	I have no choice but to melt when I look at him.
	His eyes should define how I spend my future.

Part of what makes the situation feel complicated to Ruby is that she's not taking responsibility for her choices, her values, and her desires. She's not willing to accept the consequences of being clear and honest but misses the benefits of a straightforward approach. Her desire to please everyone, including the conflicting parts of herself, is what complicates her situation.

Ruby's Rant	Thought Bank
This is so complicated. I hate that it's so complicated.	This is complicated.
	I hate that it's complicated.

Now Ruby admits to wanting to "get together" with a fantasy. As long as she's attached to an imagined dog-loving, city-dwelling Johnny, she can't accept the reality of the ex-boyfriend standing before her, the one whose desires don't align with her own.

Ruby's Rant	Thought Bank
He should just be happy living in the city and having a dog or something. I could have a dog. But no, he won't let go of his stupid rancher dream and yet keeps looking at me with those eyes.	He should be happy living in the city. A dog should be enough for him. His rancher dream is stupid. He confuses me when he looks at me. When he looks at me with those eyes, I'm no longer able to think straight.

Whenever we step out of ourselves to judge the world, others, or our own actions, we become disembodied and feel abandoned, empty, alone. This is exactly what Ruby does at the end of her Rant. She jumps into platitudes about how life and love "should be" and totally loses touch with reality.

Ruby's Rant	Thought Bank
It's just so unfair! Love should be easy. If you meet someone, and they're meant to be, then it should be easy to know, shouldn't it? Whatever happened to, "all you need is love?"	This is unfair. Life should be fair. Love should be easy. It should be easy to know if someone is meant to be. All you need is love. Love is enough to hold a relationship together.

Ruby is projecting how she might feel in the future under different circumstances. The statements below can't be captured by a camera; they're conjecture. Such beliefs are always worth investigating because they pull Ruby out of the present reality and into a movie of her own creation.

Ruby's Rant	Thought Bank
This would be so much easier if he just ran off with some other girl. Or if it turned out he was gay. Or if he had lots of acne. Then it wouldn't hurt so much.	This would be so much easier if he just ran off with some other girl. This would be so much easier if it turned out he was gay. This would be so much easier if he had lots of acne. It hurts so much because he wants to be with me. If he didn't want to be with me, it would hurt less.

In my workshops, I'll sometimes ask one participant to Rant before the group and for the others to write the thoughts they guess the speaker is believing. The more they practice culling beliefs from a Rant, the better they get at pinpointing the beliefs upsetting the speaker. They're often correct in their assumptions.

Identifying beliefs is like being able to distinguish the violins in a symphony. When my son was little and we'd listen to classical music, either at live concerts or next to our home speakers, I would occasionally ask him to close his eyes and listen carefully. Over time, his ears became attuned to hearing the violins, the cellos, the oboes. Each instrument has its musical pattern, its unique resonance, its range of notes. Similarly, people have patterns of thinking that, when you attune your ears to hearing them, become easy to identify.

When you're engaged in Journaling Inquiry, I recommend you Rant as a free-writing exercise. Get it all out. No stopping, no editing, no questioning. Put what you've written aside for at least a few minutes. Get up and stretch, use the bathroom, or grab a drink of water. Then come back and, slowly, read what you've written. As you read, begin creating a Thought Bank, considering:

1. Is this statement a fact that a camera can capture? If not, I'm expressing my judgments or beliefs.

2. If the facts disturb me, what about them is so upsetting? (e.g. It's raining. —> My wedding will be ruined.)

3. What am I assuming about myself, the others in the situation, or life?

4. Could another person perceive these circumstances differently? Then my perceptions of the situation are clearly beliefs.

5. If I could write a sentence with the words "should" "need" or "have to" about this situation, what would it be?

6. Does my Rant include questions? How can I change them into statements?

7. Am I using tenuous language? How can I clarify that statement to more directly tap into my emotions? (e.g. "Maybe they won't like me" can become "They won't like me.")

8. Do my stated desires and actions contradict each other?

9. Do my desires and beliefs contradict each other?

Once you create a Thought Bank of beliefs from your Rant, it's time to dive into Inquiry.

Ruby wanted to escape the emotional turmoil she'd sunk into. So, she listened carefully as I read my list to her. She believed every statement to be true, and they all upset her.

Chana: Which one seems the truest and simultaneously feels the most upsetting?

Ruby: I want to get back together.

Now I'll jump into Inquiry. As I explain in *Hold That Thought*, I use a mixture of Byron Katie's *The Work*, Barry Neil Kaufman's *Option Process*, and tools of my own creation. In Inquiry, we clarify what we're believing, question those beliefs, and find our way back to truth and a centered calm.

Chana: Ruby, close your eyes and imagine yourself standing at the doorway with Johnny. Is it true that you want to get back together?

Ruby: Yes.

Chana: Can you absolutely know it's true?

44

Ruby: I don't know… it's so confusing.

Chana: Take a breath and answer the question with a simple "yes" or "no." Can you absolutely know it's true that you want to get back together?

Ruby: I guess not. Not *absolutely.* I broke up with him for a reason. For a bunch of reasons, actually.

Chana: And how do you react when you believe you want to get back together?

Ruby: (tears streaming down face) I feel sad. Really sad. And I feel all muddled inside. It's like my organs have all flipped around and changed places.

Chana: Anything else?

Ruby: Yeah. My mind gets so garbled up and confused. Oh!

Chana: Why did you say that?

Ruby: I just realized that when you asked me if I absolutely knew whether I wanted to get back together that my mind got messed up in just this way. The thought itself is turning my mind into spaghetti.

Chana: What does that mean?

Ruby: It means that I thought the situation was confusing, but maybe these thoughts are making me forget what I know to be true.

Chana: What do you know to be true?

Ruby: That Johnny and I can't be together. It'll never work. At least, not the way we are now. We want different things. I mean, we could change, but right now, he's Mr. Rancher and I'm Miss City Girl. I don't want to change, and I wouldn't want him to pretend he wants something just to please me. Eventually, he'd resent me for that.

Chana: So what do you want?

Ruby: I want to be honest with myself.

Chana: How?

Ruby: First, by not believing that I want to get back together with Johnny.

Chana: What could you believe instead?

Ruby: That I *don't* want to get back together with him.

I explained to Ruby that every belief we have functions like a command to the subconscious, telling it what to look out for. Our brains then seek evidence to prove our beliefs true. Once, for example, I purchased a tie as a gift for a friend. Being a single woman, I had never paid attention to ties, but once I started looking for them, I noticed them in every shop window. Who knew there were so many ties in the world?

Ruby walked into our conversation believing she wanted to get together. Her brain, wired to seek it out, fed her supporting evidence, including Johnny's smile and flowers. But this belief makes her miserable, which is why exploring the *opposite* belief can free her. But in order for her mind to take it seriously, it needs solid support to build a strong neural connection in the brain. She can do this by offering supportive evidence of how the thought is true or truer than her original statement. She'll be convincing the jury of her mind like a defense attorney uses legal evidence to support her case in court.

Chana: Can you give me reasons why it's *more* true that you don't want to get back together?

Ruby: There's the whole city versus country thing.

Chana: What else?

Ruby: (Laughs)

Chana: Why'd you just laugh?

Ruby: This is embarrassing to say, but if I'm really honest with myself, I know I could adapt to just about anything. There've got to be things about Johnny that just don't work for me. Otherwise, I would leap into his pickup truck and move to Farmersville.

Chana: Can you guess what those things might be?

Ruby: I love going out to restaurants. Not just a little, mind you. I really, really love every moment of the experience. And Johnny thinks they're a waste of money. He only wants to cook at home and then there are all these dishes to do. It's not as fun. And out in the country, there are, like, no restaurants. And they're usually nasty diners.

Chana: What else?

Ruby: He's always reading classic books like Dostoyevsky and stuff and I'm more interested in the newspaper and politics. We end up not having much to talk about on that front. If I got pulled out of the buzz of the city, it would be even worse. Oh yeah, and it must suck here for him with everyone constantly on ticker-tape mode with the latest headlines. But…

Chana: But what?

Ruby: (Cries) He's such a great guy. And those eyes…

Chana: He's such a great guy. Is it true?

Ruby: Yes, for sure!

Chana: How about we make the language a bit more precise. If the sentence, "He's a great guy" had to have an object, what would it be?

Ruby: Hmm… He's a great guy… for…

Chana: For who?

Ruby: For… me?

Chana: Let's see if that gives you more clarity. Johnny is a great guy *for you.* Is that true?

Ruby: Oh. I guess not. As soon as you asked me that, I immediately pictured him standing in the middle of a vegetable garden, picking tomatoes… with some *other girl.*

Chana: What does that mean?

Ruby: It hadn't occurred to me to question whether he was great for me. Huh.

Chana: Why'd you say that?

Ruby: I just realized. I thought if he was a great guy, I had to hold on to him.

47

Chana: Why?

Ruby: Because there aren't enough great guys out there.

We've got new beliefs to add to Ruby's Thought Bank. The ones under the surface are often the most potent, so they're worth noting. It might even be worth shifting the entire trajectory of the Inquiry process towards these more poignant beliefs, as I'm guessing they're really at the root of Ruby's suffering.

Chana: There aren't enough guys out there for what?

Ruby: For me to find a match. Someone I'll marry. What if I end up alone?

Chana: What does that have to do with Johnny?

Ruby: Hm… well, I'm not sure.

Chana: If you had to guess, what would you say?

Ruby: Oh. Oh no.

Chana: Why did you say that?

Ruby: All this time I thought I was confused. That I wanted to get back together with Johnny.

Chana: Are you still confused?

Ruby: No. It's so much clearer now. This wasn't about Johnny. I just don't want to end up alone.

Chana: What do you want?

Ruby: I want to explore that more. The fear of being alone. Just the word "alone" makes my stomach churn.

Chana: We can Inquire about that. You don't want to be alone. Is it true?

Ruby: Yes.

Chana: Can you absolutely know that it's true?

Ruby: Absolutely? That's harder. So I guess I would say no.

Chana: And how do you react when you believe you don't want to be alone?

Ruby: My body wants to curl up in a ball. I feel small. And scared and sad. I don't want to talk to anyone.

My guess is that as a reader, you already see the irony in Ruby's logic. Her belief about being alone makes her behave in ways that make her alone. My experience facilitating hundreds of Inquiries tells me that Ruby's probably missed this obvious contradiction. So, I'm going to guide her to see it.

Chana: Ruby, what are you hoping to accomplish by believing the thought that you don't want to be alone?

Ruby: What do you mean?

Chana: Every belief we espouse is like a tool we pull out of our toolbox when we want to accomplish a certain goal. So, if I want to drive a nail into a wall, I would pull out a hammer. If this belief is the hammer, what's the nail?

Ruby: I guess I don't want to be lonely.

Chana: So, you're hoping that by believing you don't want to be alone, you'll be less lonely?

Ruby: Yes.

Chana: And what actually happens? How do you react when you believe that thought?

Ruby: Oh!

Chana: Oh what?

Ruby: How could I not have seen this? The thought itself makes me feel alone. It makes me hide from people and keep them away.

Chana: Is that how you reacted to Johnny?

Ruby: No. With him, it was the opposite. I held on to him like a puppy clinging for dear life. Ugh.

Chana: Why did you say that?

Ruby: I don't enjoy thinking of myself that way. Either reclusive or desperate.

Chana: How do you want to see yourself?

Ruby: Strong, happy, liking myself.

Chana: How does it feel to say that?

Ruby: Just saying the words makes me sit taller. I like myself more when I think of myself as strong and happy.

Chana: Let's explore the scene with Johnny with the stance you have right now. Close your eyes and imagine him at your door. And the thought that you don't want to be alone isn't there. How are you without it?

Ruby: I'm calmer. That desperate feeling in my chest is gone. I see Johnny's just scared of being alone, too. That's why he's here, even though he knows we're not a good fit. He's saying he wants to get back together, but I know it's just the fear speaking. I can love him and tell him not to come in. We don't belong together and it's okay.

Chana: How do you feel?

Ruby: So much better. The entire scene is much less complicated. It's pretty simple, really. Two people scared of being alone are clinging to each other. But it's useless.

Chana: Why?

Ruby: Because when we're together, we're technically not alone, but it still feels pretty lonely.

Chana: How?

Ruby: I can't talk about politics with him and he can't talk about his boring classics with me. See how I even relate to his books? It's pretty sad. Besides that, he's itching to move to some farm and clinging to me is keeping him in the city. He's like a fish out of water. He doesn't belong here. If I hold on to him, it's totally selfish and cruel. Like I'm just using him so I can pretend I'm not alone.

Chana: What do you want?

Ruby: I want to not cling to him. I want to be okay with being alone.

Chana: So let's explore the opposite of the thought that you don't want to be alone.

Ruby: I do want to be alone.

Chana: How's that true?

Ruby: The past couple of weeks since we broke up, I've gone out to eat like six times. I got to spend time with friends I didn't see so much when Johnny was in the picture, and I even went to Al Forno by myself. I treated myself to every appetizer on the menu and had them stagger them out so I could relish each one. Kid you not, I was there for four hours. By myself!

Chana: How do you feel about that?

Ruby: I loved it! I had so much fun. And I was alone. But I wasn't lonely.

Chana: Why?

Ruby: I guess because I was so present in the moment. I was having so much fun being a foodie. I didn't think about being alone.

Chana: How does it feel to notice that?

Ruby: Really good. I actually enjoyed it more than when I took Johnny there. He was so focused on how expensive it was and how he could make the dishes at home. It ruined the experience. Wow.

Chana: Why'd you say that?

Ruby: I was more lonely *with* Johnny than *without* him.

Chana: Can you offer more reasons you do want to be alone?

Ruby: When I'm reading a great article, I ignore everyone else in the room. In essence, I'm alone. And I'm fine. More than fine.

Chana: What else?

Ruby: I'd rather be alone and doing what I love than be with a guy I don't belong with and be lonely.

Chana: What's another opposite of the belief that you don't want to be alone?

Ruby: I don't want to be together. That's true. I don't want to be with Johnny. Not the real Johnny, the one who wants to cook and live on a farm and read classics.

Chana: How do you feel?

Ruby: Calmer. (Smiles)

Chana: Why did you smile?

Ruby: My head was all garbled up. But it's clearer now. It's such a relief. Like I can finally let go of Johnny. I can say goodbye and not be panicky. I feel more okay with being alone.

Chana: It seems to me you already were.

Ruby: I guess so. I chose to take myself to Al Forno and enjoyed it, but I ignored how great that was when Johnny came to my door. I won't forget that again.

Chana: What do you want to do?

Ruby: I want to write to him. I want to tell him it's really over. And that I believe he and I can both handle being alone. That I have faith in each of us.

Ruby's emotions were so intense and varied that she couldn't even clarify what she was thinking. Being able to share her entire story without trying to filter, analyze, or understand it helped her identify her beliefs. From this Rant, we could then build a Thought Bank that became the basis of our Inquiry.

TUNING IN

Now it's your turn to Rant. Think of a time you were upset. In your journal, write the story of what happened. Don't edit your writing; get it all out. Then put your journal down and take a break. You can drink a cup of tea, go for a walk, or read an article. Reopen your journal and below your Rant, write My Thought Bank about... (e.g.

My bicycling accident, Jane's wedding, the lady at the store.) Now read the Rant you've written. Try to identify each belief you've stated outright or implied between the lines. Add these to your Thought Bank. If you've stated a simple fact like, "He knocked on the door," but notice that it made you really mad, ask yourself, "What about his knock made me mad?" or "Why did his knock make me mad?" Add your responses to your Thought Bank. Then do a Journal Inquiry on one of your beliefs.

To learn more about **The Rant,**
access **Free Bonus Materials** at

ChanaMason.com/Inner-Voices-Bonus.

The Slow Poke

The more man meditates upon good thoughts,
the better will be his world and the world at large.

—Confucius

"I'm so upset!" Clara cried at the beginning of our session.

"Why?" I asked.

"The church ladies. They just left me in the dust."

Clara's church was running a fundraiser, and a committee gathered to organize the event. As one of the retired ladies in the congregation, Clara figured she had the time and energy to help out. She volunteered to recruit local businesses to donate prizes for their raffle, so she needed access to the church's non-profit tax receipts.

"But I couldn't reach the committee head," she said. "We were stuck in phone tag for over a week. I finally saw her in church last Sunday, and Beatrice told me she and Alice had already taken care of it. Weeks before the event!"

Clara's posture slumped, and her eyes darted around. She couldn't settle into her own skin as she told this story.

I could already guess some of her beliefs and wrote them in my notebook

> She wasted my time.
> She doesn't respect me.
> She should have called me.
> She should have kept her commitment.

Before sharing my list with Clara, I wanted to see what beliefs she could identify on her own.

"What about this is upsetting you?" I asked.

"I don't know. I'm just so uncomfortable." Clara squirmed in her seat. "I don't even want to go to the fundraiser anymore."

It was important to me we clarify exactly what was upsetting Clara. Sometimes there are so many thoughts garbled in our heads, as if multiple radio stations are playing, we can't hear a clear tune amidst the chaos. Our minds fire thousands of neural connections a minute, which can be overwhelming for us to process.

That's why I recommended Clara use The Slow Poke.

"Close your eyes and breathe," I told her, "and imagine yourself back in church last Sunday, right when Beatrice told you it was taken care of. Now imagine playing that moment in slow motion." Clara's breathing took on a steady pace as her mind focused on the memory. "There's a gap between her words and your reaction. Stretch that gap in time, Slow it down, so you can Poke right at the thoughts running through your head. What beliefs show up in that gap?"

As Clara spoke, I added her words to my notebook:

> Do they even want my help?
> I don't click with them.
> I can't work with them.
> They were supposed to do other projects with their time.
> They misused their time.
> It'll be uncomfortable at church now.
> They don't care about my opinion.

Every statement was ripe for Inquiry but one. Can you identify it? It's the first one, the question.

Chana: We can question statements, but not questions. Clara, can you turn "do they even want my help?" into a statement?

Clara: I guess I'm scared they don't want my help.

Chana: So there's your belief: "They don't want my help."

Clara: Yeah.

I added this belief to the Thought Bank and read her my list, including my original guesses.

Chana: Which of these is the most upsetting to you?

Clara: That they don't respect me. It's embarrasing, but I'm really intimidated by them. They're the most devoted ladies in the church and always look so composed.

Chana: So, they don't respect you. Is that true?

Clara: Yes.

Chana: Can you absolutely know that it's true?

Clara: Absolutely? I couldn't know that for sure.

Chana: And how does that thought make you feel?

Clara: Like they don't care about me. Like they just look down on me.

Chana: Is that what you're thinking, or how you're feeling?

Clara: What do you mean?

Chana: Feelings exist as sensations in the body. Thoughts live in the head and then lead you to have physical reactions.

Clara: Okay… so, I guess them not caring about me and looking down on me are not feelings; they're thoughts.

Chana: We'll add them to your Thought Bank as beliefs you can explore later.

> They don't care about me.
> They look down at me.

Chana: For now, let's return to your original thought. How do you feel when you're believing that they don't respect you? Check into your body. What physical sensations come up? What emotions?

Clara: Tightness. My hands clench. And I shrink back.

Chana: Anything else?

Clara: It makes me feel shy, like I don't want to look them in the eyes.

Chana: Let's do a reset. Take a deep breath and shake it all out. Close your eyes again and picture yourself back at church on Sunday. Beatrice tells you they already took care of it, but this time, the thought that they don't respect you isn't there. How are you without it?

Clara: I'm calmer. Less jittery.

Chana: Now let's turn that thought around. What's the opposite of "they don't respect you?"

Clara: They do respect me?

Chana: Yes. Can you offer some evidence for why that's true?

Clara: Beatrice actually tried to deliver the tax receipts to my house, but I wasn't around. So it wasn't like she blew me off entirely.

Chana: What else?

Clara: She chose me to be the Sunday school teacher for her twins' grade.

Chana: And…

Clara: And she was very much a part of the phone tag, also calling me and not reaching me.

Chana: You have three reasons. Do you need more?

Clara: Probably. I'm pretty attached to this belief. Oh. Here's a reason: Alice and Beatrice and I were in the same bible study group. For years. And then I had to switch groups when my schedule changed.

Chana: Take a moment to recall that group. Did they do anything to disrespect you there?

Clara: (closes her eyes) Actually, I'd be really shy around them. But they usually greeted me first. And they'd ask questions about my thoughts on what we were studying. It's just…

Chana: Just what?

Clara: I don't know...

Chana: What don't you know?

Clara: I don't really think they were being sincere.

Chana: What do you mean?

Clara: I think they were just being nice to me cause they pitied me. So they didn't act disrespectfully. But they didn't actually respect me. Really, they look down at me. It's so awkward.

Chana: Notice how, in order to believe Beatrice and Alice don't respect you, you have to believe other unkind things about them.

Clara: What do you mean?

Chana: That they're not sincere. You're basically saying they lie.

Clara: Oh.

Chana: They ask you what you think. That's a lie. They greet you. That's a lie. They welcome you to help plan the fundraiser. That's a lie.

Clara: I thought it was about me being a loser.

Chana: In order for you to make yourself a weakling, you turn them into monsters in your eyes.

Clara: That's not really how I see these ladies. They're really holy. I'm just intimidated by them.

Chana: This intimidation either makes them superhuman, in which case you can't treat them with directness. Or it makes you less than human, less worthy than them, which makes any kindness just a sign of insincere pity.

Clara: Both feel uncomfortable.

Chana: Yes. Because really, you're both craving connection. Maybe you're a whole person, with strengths and foibles, and so are they.

Clara: Don't laugh at me, but now that I think about it, I wouldn't want their lives. They've got enormous challenges. One is working crazy hours at a job she hates just to make ends meet. And the other one is battling cancer.

Chana: Not so superhuman.

Clara: No.

Chana: This brings us to the next turnaround. What's another opposite of "they don't respect me?" Let's change the subject of the sentence.

Clara: I don't respect me?

Chana: How's that true?

Clara: I make myself small when I'm around them. And I don't talk straight with them.

Chana: What do you mean?

Clara: Well, I had told Beatrice that I'm not so good at initiating things, but I like to help others out in a pinch, so if they need help with the fundraiser, I'm here for them.

Chana: In a pinch?

Clara: Not so enthusiastic, huh?

Chana: Did you actually *want* to help?

Clara: Yes!

Chana: So why didn't you just say that?

Clara: I guess I wanted to make it easy for them to say no if they didn't want me.

Chana: I think it just led them to believe you weren't so committed.

Clara: What do you mean?

Chana: How do you know someone is really excited to be with you, to do something with you?

Clara: Um… They smile. They're energetic. They follow up.

Chana: And when you talk to them, what do their eyes do?

Clara: They look right at me. In a really focused, attentive way. Oh.

Chana: Oh, what?

Clara: I don't do that. I avoid eye contact with them. I look at the floor. But that's just cause I'm intimidated.

Chana: But if you put yourself in their shoes, what do they see?

Clara: That *I'm* not so interested in *them.* Oh my. That's another turnaround. I don't respect them. But that's not true! I do!

Chana: Does your behavior show that?

Clara: Not exactly. They're always the ones to come to say "hi" to me. I avoid them when I come to church because I don't want to bother them.

Chana: If someone avoided me, I would just assume they don't like me or respect me.

Clara: Of course. Right.

Chana: So maybe there was something in your body language, your tone, your words, your behavior that led them to believe you wouldn't follow through.

Clara: I can see that.

Chana: That's the challenge of not being straight with people. When you skirt around them, they'll struggle to be straight with you. They might have just concluded it would be easier to do this task themselves than have to dance around you.

Clara: But it's sad, cause I would have done it happily.

Chana: I hear that. They missed out on your help because of it.

Clara: Right. They have so much on their plate with this fundraiser, and they took on yet another task. How overwhelming.

Chana: And how do they benefit from taking so much upon themselves?

Clara: What do you mean?

Chana: Do you ever take on more than you can chew?

Clara: Yes.

Chana: Why do you do that?

Clara: This is embarrassing, but honestly, it's because I want to see myself as exceptional. And I want other people to see me that way, too.

Chana: A lot of us struggle with that challenge. You don't think Beatrice and Alice do?

Clara: I don't know. They actually are exceptional. They're such composed ladies who get so much done. Oh. I see.

Chana: What do you see?

Clara: I don't know what's going on inside their heads. Maybe they do so much not because they're superhuman, but because they want everyone else to *think* they are.

Chana: And how does it make you feel when you do that?

Clara: It's exhausting.

Chana: Do you respect yourself - your body, your needs - when you do that?

Clara: No. I push myself too hard. I commit to too much. Maybe that's what they thought I'd done. Maybe they thought I was over-committed. And they didn't want to burden me with that.

Chana: So perhaps they were trying to be kind.

Clara: Yes. Beatrice actually said a number of times, "If it's too much for you, don't worry, we can do it." But I said, "No, it's no problem."

Chana: It's no problem?

Clara: That's the language of someone who's feeling burdened but wants to show that she can handle it.

Chana: Is that true?

Clara: No. I really wanted to help. I was just being shy, I guess.

Chana: Intimidated.

Clara: Yeah.

Chana: What do you think about that now?

Clara: I just keep imagining all of us overextending ourselves and misreading each other. It's sad. And I pity that they're taking on too much.

Chana: Do you still want to avoid going to church?

Clara: No. I can see them as human now.

Chana: So what do you want?

Clara: I want to help.

Chana: Can you just tell them that?

Clara: What if they don't want me?

Chana: What if you trusted them to be honest?

Clara: You mean that if they didn't want me, they would just say so?

Chana: Yes.

Clara: But that's rude. They wouldn't do that.

Chana: So they'd lie.

Clara: Oh. Right. It's either honesty or dishonesty.

Chana: Yes. Those are your choices.

Clara: I'd rather see them as honest. And if in the end, they're not, it's their problem.

Chana: They'll have to face the consequences.

Clara: Yeah. Wow. I never realized how mean-spirited I've been.

Chana: How so?

Clara: I always assume that when people are nice to me, they don't mean it. They're either putting me down or buttering me up to get something. Oh dear. It's like I make everyone slimy.

Chana: How might you avoid that?

Clara: By just trusting people.

Chana: Can you do that?

Clara: Yes. I can. Because really, I believe in my heart that people are good.

Chana: How can you remind yourself of this?

Clara: I could put something on my fridge, like a magnet with a quote from the Bible about honesty. And I could call Beatrice and be honest with her about my desire to help. And in my head, I tell myself she's also being honest.

Chana: Why'd you just grin?

Clara: I like this. I like the way it feels to trust people. There's a part of me that finds it scary, but here, in my chest, it feels warm.

Clara struggled in her interactions with women she highly respected at her church but couldn't figure out what upset her so much. Using The Slow Poke helped her stretch time and see the thoughts running through her mind. She believed the ladies didn't respect her because she didn't see herself as worthy. This led her to withdraw and see them in a twisted light. Inquiry helped her be more compassionate towards these women and see them as equals.

TUNING IN

Now it's your turn to practice The Slow Poke. Think of a time you felt overwhelmed with emotion and unable to identify the cause of your upset. Close your eyes and picture that moment stretching as if you're playing the scene in slow motion. What were you believing about your circumstances that led you to react the way you did? Write your answers in your journal. Then do a Journal Inquiry on at least one of the beliefs. The more thoughts you question, the more you'll free your mind!

The Cipher

> *We are addicted to our thoughts.*
> *We cannot change anything*
> *if we cannot change our thinking.*
>
> —*Santosh Kalwar*

Gordon had an idea for a novel he believed would excite publishers. He was eager to write Addie's Adventures, a story about a kid on a globe-trotting escapade, and had already developed details for it in his head. He'd never been so passionate about a book before, and it meant a lot to him.

So, as you might guess, he hadn't written a word.

Gordon: I'm just too busy.

Chana: Too busy?

Gordon: Well, things just keep coming up. Other projects. Other books. I don't know.

Chana: What don't you know?

Gordon: I don't think I'll be able to write Addie as well as I want to. I mean, I've never been a super successful author. I'm just not making fast enough progress at being a self-published author. What makes me think a publisher would go for Addie? Really, I'm just scared to even outline the thing. Every time I even think about the book, my heart starts to race. It's so embarrassing. I should have already finished Addie; it was supposed to have been done this summer.

As Gordon delivered his Rant, I wrote a Thought Bank from what he clearly stated or implied.

The Rant is so immensely central to the work I do with clients (and the work we all do in our journals,) that I want to cover it more slowly here.

Before we jump into my list, let's clarify how I go about deciphering a

Rant into a Thought Bank. Whenever I break down a Rant, I follow these Cipher *rules*:

1. **Facts don't belong in a Thought Bank. If the statement could be captured by a camera, it's a fact. Otherwise, the Rant is reflecting judgments or beliefs.**

    e.g. "The train arrived an hour late" is a fact. "The conductor was irresponsible" is a belief.

2. **We don't question facts, but rather, our story about the facts. So, if a fact is upsetting you, then ask, "What about this upsets me?" or "What does this mean?"**

    e.g. "I was late for work." —> "I'm going to lose my job."

    e.g. "John didn't send me a birthday present." —> "John doesn't love me."

3. **Feelings don't belong in a Thought Bank**

    e.g. "I feel sad" or "my head hurts" are feelings (or physical sensations.)

4. **Statements that begin with "I feel" are often thoughts, not feelings.**

    e.g. "I feel that he's being unfair." = "He's being unfair."

    e.g. "I feel cheated." = "She's cheating me."

    e.g. "I feel lonely." is a feeling. "I feel alone." = "I am alone."

    (For a complete list of feeling words, go here: https://www.cnvc. org/training/resource/feelings-inventory)

5. **We question statements, not questions. So, questions need to be turned into statements.**

    e.g. "Why is this happening to me?" —> "This shouldn't be happening to me."

    e.g. "Why does everyone hate me?" —> "Everyone hates me."

6. **Include assumptions or *rules* of life that cause you distress. Though you can support them with loads of scientific research, they may nonetheless be limiting you.**

   e.g. "Women are more sensitive than men." (And that's why I can't relate to them.)

   e.g. "Smoking is bad for you." (And I, therefore, can't tolerate when others smoke.)

7. **Make tenuous words into direct language that taps into your emotions.**

   e.g. "I might not make it." —> "I won't make it."

8. **If the actions of the Ranter are in contradiction to their stated desire, add the desire to the Thought Bank.**

   e.g. Someone who's been gaining 20 kilos each year and doesn't exercise claims, "I want to lose weight."

9. **If the desires of the Ranter are in contradiction to their beliefs, add the desire to the Thought Bank.**

   e.g. Someone who belongs to a strictly Catholic community says, "I want to live a gay lifestyle."

10. **It's worthwhile guessing from what's said between the lines. The Ranter will correct you if necessary. (My students do a great job at making these guesses, so don't hold back.)**

    e.g. "Dan hasn't called. We went out two weeks ago, and he still hasn't called. Why do I have to be so ugly?" —> "Dan should have called," "He didn't call because I'm ugly," "I'm not pretty enough to get a guy."

11. **Write sentences with the words "should" "need" or "have to" implied by the Rant.**

    e.g. "Jane isn't listening to me. How could I get through this wedding if she doesn't listen to me? She's not doing her job as Maid of Honor." —> "Jane should listen to me," "I need Jane to listen to me," "A Maid of Honor has to listen to the bride."

In short form, the Cipher rules are:

1. Facts don't belong in a Thought Bank.

2. Identify the meaning you attach to facts.

3. Feelings don't belong in a Thought Bank.

4. Identify thoughts preceded by "I feel."

5. Turn questions into statements.

6. Add upsetting assumptions or rules.

7. Make statements clear and direct.

8. Add desires to the Thought Bank that contradict actions.

9. Add desires to the Thought Bank that contradict beliefs.

10. Guess what's being implied.

11. Add "should"s, "need"s, or "have to"s implied by the Rant.

Now let's take a look at Gordon's Rant:

I'm just too busy. Well, things just keep coming up. Other projects. Other books.

Rules Applied to Gordon's Rant	Thought Bank
Question assumptions.	I'm too busy.
Guess what's being implied.	Things keep coming up.
Add desires to the Thought Bank that contradict actions.	My other books and projects are keeping me too busy.
	I want to write Addie's Adventures.

I don't know.

Rules I Applied to his Rant	My Thought Bank
Question assumptions. (I'm guessing he simply doesn't want to know.)	I don't know. I don't know why I'm not working on Addie. I don't know what's wrong. I don't know what's holding me back.

I don't think I'll be able to write Addie as well as I want to. I mean, I've never been a super successful author. I'm just not making fast enough progress at being a self-published author.

Rules I Applied to his Rant	My Thought Bank
Guess what's being implied. Add "should"s, "need"s, or "have to"s implied by the Rant. Add desires to the Thought Bank that contradict beliefs.	I won't be able to write Addie as well as I want to. I should write Addie well. I need to write better for a publisher than I write for myself. I've never been a super successful author. I need to be a super successful author in order to write Addie. I need to be a super successful author in order to get picked up by a publisher. I'm not making fast enough progress at being a self-published author. I want to pitch Addie to a publisher.

What makes me think a publisher would go for Addie?

Rules I Applied to his Rant	My Thought Bank
Turn questions into statements	A publisher won't go for Addie.
	It's crazy to think a publisher would go for Addie.
	I have no reason to think a publisher would go for Addie

Really, I'm just scared to even outline the thing. Every time I even think about the book, my heart starts to race. It's so embarrassing. I should have already finished Addie; it was supposed to have been done this summer.

Rules I Applied to his Rant	My Thought Bank
Feelings don't belong in a Thought Bank.	I'm too scared to outline the book.
Question assumptions. (Every time, really?)	Every time I think about the book, my heart starts to race.
Guess what's being implied.	I can't think about the book.
Add "should"s, "need"s, or "have to"s implied by the Rant.	It's too hard to outline.
	I should have already finished Addie.
	Addie should have been done this summer.

Chana: Which of these beliefs most upsets you?

Gordon: I felt a ton of pressure in my chest when you read, "I need to write better for a publisher than I write for myself." It feels so true, and it's crushing.

Chana: Other than the pressure in your chest, how do you react when you believe that?

Gordon: Sad. Like my future is hopeless.

Chana: Imagine sitting at your desk to write, what happens?

Gordon: I can't write. I can just do mundane tasks like paying bills and responding to emails. I've got no creative juice.

Chana: So you can't even write at the level you usually write for yourself.

Gordon: Yeah. It's sad.

Chana: Close your eyes and picture yourself at your desk again. Take a deep breath and, as you exhale, imagine blowing out the thought that you need to write better for a publisher than you do for yourself. See it floating out the window. How are you now?

Gordon: Calmer. I can just focus on writing the story. It's interesting…

Chana: What is?

Gordon: When I write for myself, I just write. Sometimes the writing is better, sometimes less so. But even when I think a book is fantastic, that doesn't mean that kids are going to love it. And this one book I published last year was a hit, even though I wasn't so hot about it.

Chana: What does that tell you?

Gordon: I'm not sure I would know how to "write for a publisher."

Chana: No wonder you're not trying.

Gordon: Yeah. It seems like an impossible task. I can only write what I write; and in the end, it's either great or not, but in the process of writing, I can't know.

Chana: This supports the turnaround that you don't need to write better for a publisher than you do for yourself. What's another reason?

Gordon: My books are selling already, so something in my writing is resonating with readers.

Chana: What else?

Gordon: If a publisher doesn't buy the book, I can still publish it myself.

Chana: Do you hear the irony in what you just said?

Gordon: No. What?

Chana: What's the definition of a publisher?

Gordon: A company that publishes books. Why?

Chana: Think about it...

Gordon: Oh wait... I never thought of it that way. *I'm a publisher.* I publish books.

Chana: Yep. And how many of your books have been financial flops?

Gordon: None, actually. They're all profitable. Wait... are you implying that my little business is actually a successful publisher?

Chana: Is that what *you're* implying?

Gordon: I guess I am. Huh...

Chana: What?

Gordon: I thought one of the big five publishers had to buy my books in order to think of myself as a successful author. But looking at it this way, I'm already a successful author.

Chana: And a successful publisher.

Gordon: Yes.

Chana: Do you still want to go with a big five publisher?

Gordon: Honestly, yes. For Addie, it would be cool. They have distribution in schools and libraries I don't have access to.

Chana: How does it feel to say that?

Gordon: It doesn't sound stressful. It sounds like fun. I'd like to work with them. It would be a challenge and an adventure, but it doesn't have that same pressure as before. They're not as big and scary now. And I don't *need* them. I'm already doing well without them.

Chana: What do you want to do?

Gordon: I want to write Addie. I'm excited about his story, and I don't want to put it off anymore. It's a great idea.

Chana: How can you take action to make sure that happens?

Gordon: I can dedicate two hours a day to writing. First thing in the morning when my mind is the clearest.

Chana: Will you do that?

Gordon: Yes. I'm putting it in my calendar right now. This is exciting! I can feel a buzz in my body. I'm eager to start!

Gordon couldn't engage with his latest book idea because he felt too much pressure to write it perfectly. Questioning his beliefs about himself as an author and about big publishers helped to calm his nerves and reinvigorate his desire to write Addie's Adventures.

TUNING IN

Rant into your journal about something that has upset you recently. Take a break from your Rant, then reread it slowly, following the Cipher rules to identify the beliefs you've stated outright or implied. Once you've collected a complete Thought Bank, choose the thought that most agitates you and engage in a Journal Inquiry with it.

To learn more about **The Cipher**,
access **Free Bonus Materials** at
ChanaMason.com/Inner-Voices-Bonus.

FEELING THE VOICE

The voice within is what I'm married to.

- Byron Katie

The Tuning Fork

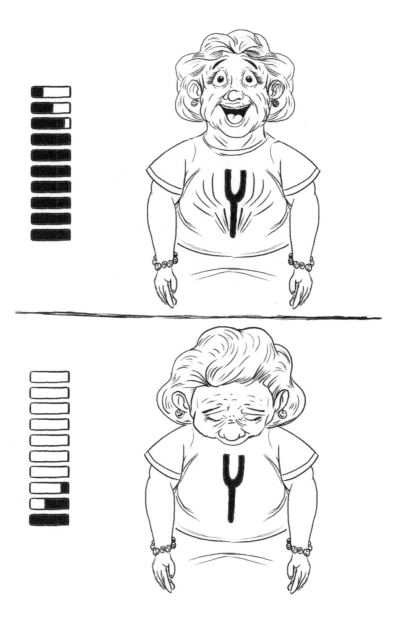

Your inner voice is the voice of divinity.
To hear it, we need to be in solitude,
even in crowded places.

— A. R. Rahman

Nigel came to me with a heavy stride and slumped posture, saying, "things just aren't working." His online retail business was growing, but his personal life was suffering.

Nigel: It hit me the other day over dinner. I was in the middle of responding to a customer's message when my five-year-old grabbed my head and turned it to face his. He stared me in the eyes and said, "Daddy! Get off your phone!" The crazy thing is that I sell healthy lifestyle products: yoga mats, meditation courses, essential oils!

Chana: What's crazy about that?

Nigel: I don't actually mean crazy. I guess I mean ironic. Here I am trying to help people live more balanced lives, yet I'm working such crazy hours. My own son has to tell me to stop.

Chana: What about that upsets you?

Nigel: I guess I feel like a hypocrite. Something's off.

Chana: What does "off" feel like for you?

Nigel: I guess unsettled. Like I can't seem to sit still. I haven't meditated in what…? Weeks… at least. I'm selling meditation pillows, for goodness sake! Things just aren't working.

Have you ever taken a UCF (Unidentified Container of Food) out of the fridge and not recalled who put it there or when? How would you know if it was edible? If you're like most non-adolescent males, you wouldn't just eat it and hope for the best, right?

You'd give the package a good sniff. And if that food made your face tighten and recoil, it'd be time to chuck the UCF into the garbage.

Whether you're in Pakistan or Paris, Bali or Bermuda, the ability to identify rotting foods using our noses is universal. But it's not the only physiological tool we have available to us.

Our bodies constantly communicate about whether we're safe or someone we meet is reliable. Many of us can sense when a storm is brewing or when someone we love is about to call. In the West, we tend to regard the intellect as the seat of all-knowing. We tend to live from the neck up. This explains why many of my clients and students struggle to notice how their bodies feel, unless they've become ill.

They miss out on all the nuanced signals their subconscious is sending them. Because, unlike the conscious mind, which communicates through words , our subconscious communicates through physical sensation. That's why you'll "get a gut feeling" about something. How you'll just "know" that someone's a good candidate for a job. How you can just "tell" that Janice and Jane will be the best of friends.

You can take advantage of this communication channel as a guide to identify what's true from what's false. Your body functions like a Tuning Fork, ringing happily when you're believing what's true, and getting off-key and constricted when you're believing a falsehood.

You can test this out easily by trying out two beliefs, one which you know to be a fact about you and the other, a fiction. So, for example, I could test out "I'm a woman" vs. "I'm a man" or "my name is Chana" vs. "my name is Maxine." For a few seconds, close your eyes and sincerely believe each statement, perhaps by repeating it over and over. How does your body react? Does it open up and relax? Does it tighten and recoil?

(WARNING: if, for example, you have a lot of negative beliefs about being a woman and you test "I'm a woman," you might be unconsciously loading "I'm too fat" or "I'm not feminine enough" or "women are second-class citizens" onto the simple fact of your being a woman, in which case you might tense up, but it would be due to these *additional beliefs*.)

Nigel's body was singing an off-key melody. And because the body's a Tuning Fork, it'll let you know when your thinking is dysfunctional. For Nigel, unhappiness was his cue.

Chana: When you say "things aren't working," what do you mean?

Nigel: My life. I feel like a hypocrite. I sell products that support healthy living, yet I can't muster the discipline to live in a healthy way.

Chana: So you believe you're suffering from a lack of discipline?

Nigel: I guess.

Chana: You guess?

Nigel: Well, when it comes to my business, I'm hyper-disciplined. I'm up until three in the morning some nights, plugging away. But...

Chana: But what?

Nigel: But for my own health, going to bed at that hour is killing me.

Chana: So is a lack of discipline your problem?

Nigel: A lack of discipline in my personal life, I guess. Something tells me you don't think so, though.

Chana: Why do you say that?

Nigel: Well, because you look confused, I guess.

Chana: I am confused. You're saying you lack discipline, and you're saying you have tons of discipline. It's a bit of a contradiction. Discipline is a muscle. You're not lacking for it. It seems to me you're just directing it in certain areas in your life and not others.

Nigel: So maybe it's not discipline, maybe it's motivation?

Chana: Let's take a look at what drives your behavior. Close your eyes and picture that dinner where your son grabbed your face. Go back to the moment before you picked up the phone to respond to your customer's message.

Nigel: Okay. I'm there. I'm already feeling antsy.

Chana: Let's ask The One Question. What are you believing in that moment that's making you feel antsy?

Nigel: There's so much pressure. I feel lazy if I'm not working. The success of this business is 100% on me.

Chana: Anything else?

Nigel: Yes. I'm trying to picture myself turning off my phone. And it stresses me out. It's like I'm wasting my time. I should be working on my business.

Chana: Why?

Nigel: It seems like anytime I'm not working on my business is wasted time.

Chana: And at that moment, when you see the customer's message, how do you relate to sleep or meditation or your boys?

Nigel: I just feel like I don't have time for them. This feels so much more important.

As Nigel spoke, I collected a Thought Bank of beliefs he was either stating outright or implying.

Nigel's Words	My Thought Bank
There's so much pressure. I feel lazy if I'm not working. The success of this business is 100% on me.	My wife is pressuring me. My customers are pressuring me. I am lazy if I'm not working. The success of this business is 100% on me.
It seems like anytime I'm not working on my business is wasted time.	Anytime I'm not working on my business is wasted time.
I'm trying to picture myself turning off my phone. And it stresses me out. It's like I'm wasting my time. I should be working on my business.	Turning off my phone stresses me out. I'm wasting my time. I should be working on my business.
I just feel like I don't have time for them. This feels so much more important.	I don't have time for meditation/sleep/my boys. My business is more important than meditation/sleep/my boys.

I read the Thought Bank to Nigel and asked him to pick the belief that felt the most true and also the most gut-wrenching.

Nigel: Probably that anytime I'm not working on my business is wasted time.

Chana: Can you see how that belief, rather than a lack of discipline, might be driving your choices?

Nigel: For sure.

Chana: Let's go back to that moment at dinner. Your son is sitting next to you, and your phone is buzzing.

Nigel: Okay. I'm there.

Chana: Is it true that anytime you're not working on your business is wasted time?

Nigel: It's embarrassing to say, but yeah. It feels really true.

Chana: Can you absolutely know that it's true?

Nigel: Honestly? I want to say yes to that.

Chana: Honesty is the goal here.

Nigel: So, yes. It just feels like I have to use everything I've got to make this thing succeed.

Chana: And how do you react - as you're sitting at the dinner table - when you believe the thought that anytime you're not working on your business is wasted time?

Nigel: My legs get jittery. I'm on edge, like a drug addict craving a hit. And everything tenses up.

Chana: Anything else?

Nigel: My mind is racing, trying to think of all the things I've got to do.

Chana: What are you unable to do when you believe that thought?

Nigel: I can't relax. And my kids feel like a distraction. It's sad to say, but they annoy me when I'm believing that. (Cries.) And really, they're such great kids...

Chana: Why are you crying?

Nigel: I love my boys so much. Believing this is ruining that. It's making me miss out on their childhoods. Like my body's at the table, but I'm not really there. Danny is trying to tell me about his latest skateboard antics, but I'm not really listening. I guess that's why he grabbed my face. That sucks. That's not the kind of Dad I want to be.

Chana: It's painful to be living contrary to your values.

Nigel: Yeah.

Chana: But look at the innocence of your behavior. Could anyone act differently believing that time away from their business is wasted?

Nigel: I guess not. It's too strong. It's so much pressure. Wait!

Chana: What?

Nigel: I just realized. I kept saying there's so much pressure. But I don't have a boss. I *am the boss*. The pressure is all from the belief. It's like this huge weight on my shoulders.

Chana: So why do you believe it?

Nigel: I guess cause I want my business to succeed. I'm scared it won't otherwise.

Chana: Let's test that out. Imagine yourself sitting at your desk. It's 2 am and you're believing that anytime you're not working on your business is wasted. How do you feel then?

Nigel: Same. Still tense. So much pressure.

Chana: How clear is your thinking?

Nigel: It's scattered. And kind of cloudy.

Chana: Creativity?

Nigel: Not much. I'm too tense for that.

Chana: Focus?

Nigel: I get distracted. Actually, just thinking the thought makes me want to check my messages. And I keep forgetting things. So sometimes I have to do double work or backtrack.

You might notice that adding work time and pressure decreases Nigel's productivity. But he might need help putting those pieces together. Realizing he's Missing the Target can help him let this belief go and consider other perspectives.

Chana: So, do you still think that to succeed in business you need this belief that anytime you're not working is wasted?

Nigel: Oh. I get it. No. It's making me *less* successful. I get it now. But…

Chana: But what?

Nigel: I mean, going back to the message I got from the customer during dinner. If I don't write him back right away, I might lose him. That's scary.

Chana: Try turning that around.

Nigel: If I write him back I might lose him?

Chana: How's that true?

Nigel: That's hard. I'm so attached to believing customers need answers right away.

Chana: Perhaps it'll help if you fully immerse yourself in that moment. Close your eyes and imagine yourself at the dinner table. How might it be true that if you write him back, you might lose him?

Nigel: Okay. I see one reason. When I'm texting on my phone, I make more typos, especially with auto-correct. I've made some embarrassing blunders there. Also, during dinner, I'm not fully focused, so I'm more likely to misunderstand the customer or miscommunicate.

Chana: Anything else?

Nigel: I guess if I burn out from working so hard, I won't be able to run my business at all. So I might keep *this specific* customer, but lose out on future ones.

Chana: Close your eyes again and imagine this dinner scene playing out over and over for the next decade. How's it true that if you write the customer back, you'll lose him?

Nigel: This is so sad. I'm seeing my boys losing interest in me and walking away from the table. And then my wife. And I'm so focused on my phone, I don't even notice until it's too late. I'll lose them. I'll lose him. I'll lose my son. And if that happens, I won't care about my customers. In which case, I'll lose them too.

Chana: Now that you've gotten more clarity on that, let's return to your original belief. Anytime you're not working is wasted. What's the opposite?

Nigel: Anytime I'm not working is not wasted.

Chana: How's that true?

Nigel: I'm either spending time with people I love or taking care of my health or my spiritual life. That's really important to me. It's not a waste.

Chana: How else is it true?

Nigel: Well, I saw before how unfocused I've gotten. I'm probably getting diminishing returns the more hours I put in. And I'm wasting all this time being on social media, but because I'm on my computer, I'm deluding myself into thinking I'm busy, but it's really just busy work.

Chana: Anything else?

Nigel: I remember reading about how Einstein got his best ideas while playing the violin. He wasn't a professional violinist, it's just something he did for pleasure, but that free time actually fueled his work as a physicist. I think if I gave myself more space to rest and play, my business could benefit.

Chana: I think this leads us to another turnaround. Can you identify an opposite for "wasted" in positive, inspiring language? Anytime you're not working on the business…

Nigel: I think I have something good. Anytime I'm not working on the business is time I'm aligning myself.

Chana: Tell me about that.

Nigel: I want to practice what I preach. It's important that my business make money but also reflect my values. So that could be every aspect of the business, including how it treats employees and what it expects from them. That means healthy eating and sleeping and for sure meditation and yoga.

Chana: How could you implement that?

Nigel: Firstly, I could gather my team and talk about these values. We could have an accountability system where everyone checks in daily. We could have metrics for exercise and meditation, not just their sales numbers or project reports. I like that. It feels more honest, and I'm getting to be myself in my business, not just some hamster in a wheel.

Chana: What else can you do?

Nigel: I could set house rules, like no phones at the table, and ask my kids to help me stick to that commitment.

Chana: And how can you tangibly make sure you meet your mediation and exercise goals?

Nigel: Hmm… that's harder. I always seem to have other things I have to do.

Chana: That's why we've got to schedule what's important to us, to make sure it happens.

Nigel: I hear that. Okay, let me think about what's realistic. So I drive my kids to school in the morning before I even begin my workday. That would be a good time… before the calls and emails start coming in. I could stop at the park on the way home and go for a run and then sit and meditate on a park bench. Wow. Just picturing that feels good.

Chana: Why?

Nigel: I can see myself getting into alignment. And my mind gets clear from the run. Then the meditation can help me further focus my mind. I could see myself energized after that to have a really productive morning at my desk. This is great.

Chana: And to further ingrain this new belief, you can say it out loud. Each time you invest in your relationships or your health, you can say, "Anytime I'm not working on the business is time I'm aligning myself."

Nigel: Like a mantra?

Chana: Yes. You can continuously program into your brain a new way of thinking about time and work.

Nigel: I think I'll write a few post-it notes and put them around the house to remind myself. Cause I might forget.

Chana: You might.

Nigel: And then what?

Chana: Your body will let you know.

Nigel: I'll get antsy again.

Chana: Exactly. And if you listen, it'll bring you back to what you already know to be true.

Nigel: That being aligned is the most important thing for me and my business. Especially if I'm thinking about the long-term success of both.

Nigel's heaviness was a gift, showing how he was living in contradiction with his highest values. Listening to his Tuning Fork, his jittery legs and tense muscles, led him to ask The One Question and identify the beliefs causing his distress. He saw how time spent away from his business brought him more in alignment with himself and could lead him to run a more sustainable and thus successful business.

TUNING IN

Check in with your own body. Slowly scan it from the top of your head to the tips of your toes. Is there any place that feels tense or uncomfortable? If so, ask yourself The One Question: What am I believing that's making me feel this way? Alternatively, close your eyes and think of a time you felt, in some way, out of sorts. Do a body scan and notice what notes your physiology is playing. How do the tension and stress manifest? Ask yourself The One Question and engage in Journal Inquiry. Be aware of how your body responds to Question 4 and to the turnarounds you create. Use these before and after metrics to further deepen your understanding of your body's signals.

If you'd like to further explore your reactions to beliefs, especially if you're facilitating others in a clinical setting, check out *The Experience Buffet* chapter in my book *Hold That Thought*, where I share a multitude of questions you can ask during Question 3 of The Work.

The Lie Detector

> *A lie gets halfway around the world before the truth has a chance to get its pants on.*
>
> —*Winston Churchill*

A ndres came to me in the hopes that a more peaceful mindset might lead to better rest. He kept waking up at three in the morning with a racing heart and couldn't get back to sleep. A few weeks of this was leading him down a spiral of exhaustion and mood swings.

Andres: I have to read every brief twice because I'm so tired, it's hard to focus. And you know how long and tedious briefs are? I just don't want to get so strung up every night.

Chana: When you wake up, is there a specific topic on your mind?

Andres: Yeah. Something I'm stressing about, trying to work out. Or something I regret.

I'm trying to get Andres to root himself in specifics, but he's speaking in generalities. Inquiry works best when we can root ourselves in a specific moment in time.

Chana: Like what?

Andres: Recently it's this stupid home remodeling gig. I'm putting new cabinets in our kitchen, and it's been a mess with the store.

Chana: What do you mean by a "mess?"

Andres: Well, I ordered these high-end cabinets from a manufacturer here in Mexico. When they came to do the measurements, it seems they got something wrong, because when the cabinets came, they didn't fit right.

Chana: What about that upsets you?

Andres: What about that doesn't upset me? Do you have any idea how much I've committed to spending on these?

Chana: So it's the money that's upsetting you?

Andres: Of course. But not just that. I went to the store and brought it up with the manager. He heard my frustrations and committed to taking care of it by the end of next week.

Chana: And that upsets you because....?

Andres: Because what if he doesn't keep his promise?

Chana: So you're concerned he won't keep his promise. Does that upset you more or less than the prospect of losing your money?

Andres: Hmm... Probably more. The idea that someone would cheat me really bothers me.

Chana: Alright. So let's Inquire about that. What's the manager's name?

Andres: Juan.

Chana: Juan won't keep his promise. Is it true?

Andres: Yes. Feels true.

Chana: Can you absolutely know that it's true?

Andres: Absolutely...? I don't know.

Chana: There's no right answer here; it's either a yes or a no.

Andres: Then no, I can't know for sure.

Chana: Now picture yourself talking to him in the store. How do you react when you believe he's not going to keep his promise?

Andres: Lousy. I can already feel my heart speeding up. And I'm getting hot. Red angry hot.

Chana: What happens to your breathing?

Andres: It gets shallow and fast. And tight. Everything is tight, actually.

Chana: What do you mean by everything?

Andres: My muscles. All over my body. Even my hands and toes are clenched.

Chana: And your stomach?

Andres: It's all tight. In my imagination, it just looks like a wall.

I explained to Andres that he had the typical collection of symptoms our bodies manifest as a result of a cascade of adrenal hormones. You may have heard of the fight—flight—freeze response that we go into when we're in danger. That response is facilitated mainly by your wee little adrenal glands, which rest right above your kidneys. So, if you're hiking through a forest and suddenly come upon a wild bear, your body quickly finds a way to get you out of this immediate danger. To do so, a number of physiological changes come into play:

1. Your breathing goes shallow to enable a much faster influx of oxygen.

2. Your heart rate speeds up to enable more blood flow - and thus oxygen and sugar - into your muscles and brain.

3. Your muscles tighten so they're ready for action.

4. Digestion shuts down - who needs to worry about lunch when you've got a life-or-death situation to manage? For many of us, this means diarrhea or constipation.

5. Your immune system shuts down - what's a virus compared to a wild bear?

6. Your vision gets narrow - you lose peripheral vision (and thus your memory and creative faculties.)

Chana: But it's not only in cases of imminent danger that we react this way. We do the exact same thing when we lie.

Andres: Really? Are you telling me that I'm lying?

Chana: If we hooked you up to a Lie Detector test, how would it react to your believing that Juan won't keep his promise?

Andres: Don't they measure heart rate or something?

Chana: Yes. And they usually check for changes in breathing or blood pressure, sometimes for sweaty palms.

Andres: I didn't even mention sweaty palms. But yeah. That's me. Sweaty everything when I wake up all stressed in the middle of the night.

Chana: So what would the Lie Detector do?

Andres: Go bonkers? Wait. So that means I'm lying? But I'm not. I really do believe that Juan might mess with me.

Chana: You might believe it, but nonetheless, your body is telling you it's false.

Andres: So if I get stressed out, that means I'm believing something that's not true?

Chana: Exactly. It's your body's warning signal, telling you to question your thinking. Now that we've done that, let's explore some different perspectives that might bring you more peace. What's the opposite of Juan won't keep his promise?

Andres: Juan will keep his promise.

Chana: How's that as true or truer than your original statement?

Andres: He said he would call me to confirm, and he did. So far, he's kept that promise. He seems like a nice guy… Um… I can't think of anything else.

Chana: Let's look at the "as true" part of my question. When will you know if he's kept his promise?

Andres: In a few weeks.

Chana: So you're predicting someone's behavior in the future. Someone you only just met.

Andres: I get it… He might keep his promise or might not. It's a toss up.

Chana: How does it feel to recognize that?

Andres: More open. I can breathe. I was so certain. But now I see why my body was so stressed. I'm not even remotely psychic. Yet I was believing my fears about the future as though they were facts.

Chana: And also, if you're honest with yourself, what's more likely: that he keeps his promise or breaks it?

Andres: I don't know.

Chana: How long has this shop been in business?

Andres: Since the 40s.

Chana: If they didn't keep their promises, what would happen?

Andres: They'd have a lot of unhappy customers.

Chana: And then what would happen?

Andres: I would've seen a ton of trash talk online. But their reviews are actually great.

Chana: So, what does that tell you about their word?

Andres: I hadn't thought of it that way. Their word is probably golden. Wow, I feel like a hundred bricks just rolled off my shoulders.

Chana: Let's take a look at another turnaround. Give me another opposite of Juan won't keep his promise. Let's put you as the subject.

Andres: I won't keep my promise? But that's ridiculous!

Chana: Before you jump to reject it, let's see if there's something you can learn here. If you're focused on keeping your promises in this business relationship, what do you commit to?

Andres: I'm committed to paying when I get a good product. And then actually enjoying the product.

Chana: How does that feel?

Andres: It's funny, but I hadn't even given a thought to *enjoying* the cabinets. All this tension might have ruined them for me, even if they were done well. It's as if they would've been packed with resentment or something. But I picked them out and paid for them. I might as well be happy with them once they're installed.

Chana: And what promises do you want to keep in your relationship with Juan?

Andres: I should say thanks to Juan and his team if they do a good job and fix the errors. I feel taller just saying I would do that. Huh...

Chana: Why'd you just say that?

Andres: Before I was feeling defensive towards him, but now I'm looking at him as a partner in my cabinet project. That feels more honest to the situation.

Chana: Turns out he's not your enemy after all.

Andres: Not at all. Poor guy, I'd made him out to be the bad guy, when he's only been responsive and helpful.

Chana: What do you want to do?

Andres: I think I should write him a message and say thanks. He's already being a great guy and I haven't acknowledged that. I bet that would also encourage him to keep his promise that much more. It's easier to keep promises to people who are nice to you.

Chana: Anything else?

Andres: I think I want to trust the guy until he proves otherwise. All this tension is exhausting!

Andres was losing sleep over an unknown future he couldn't predict, and it was ruining his ability to look forward to and eventually enjoy his new cabinets. Realizing his body was calling him out on his falsehood helped him recognize it was time to take a different perspective, one that would put him back in the driver's seat rather than leaving him the victim of his circumstances.

TUNING IN

Now it's your turn to test out The Lie Detector. Write down a list of simple facts about yourself. You might include your name, gender, place of residence, favorite food, etc. Then write a list of blatant lies about yourself. These might simply be the opposites of the first list. Pick a phrase from one list and run it through your mind. Take note of what happens to your physiology:

1. Is your heart rate fast or slow?

2. Is your breathing shallow or deep?

3. Are your muscles tight or loose?

4. Does your posture want to be collapsed or upright?

5. Is your digestion tight or smooth?

6. Is your vision blurry/tunneled or clear?

7. Do you feel weak or energetic?

You might not experience a shift in all of these physiological markers, which is fine. Most people feel a difference in at least a few. Each of these markers indicates you're either believing a falsehood or a truth. By testing it out on simple statements that don't usually confuse you, you can then trust the same principles apply to the beliefs in your Thought Bank.

The Bear Trap

> *If you hear a voice within you say 'you*
> *cannot paint,' then by all means paint,*
> *and that voice will be silenced.*
>
> —*Vincent Van Gogh*

Olivia's marriage was on the rocks. She'd only tied the knot two months prior but didn't think the relationship could last.

Olivia: It's like I can't do anything right.

Chana: What do you mean?

Olivia: Well, like the other day—this is going to sound stupid—I made pasta, and it overcooked and got all mushy. And the tomato sauce got burnt. I served it anyway, cause I was tired already. And Rob made a face when he took his first bite. I asked him if he liked it and he said, "It's fine." And I got all defensive and somehow it turned into this big fight. I ended up running out of the house.

Chana: What about that situation upsets you?

Olivia: If we're going to fight all the time, how can our marriage last? I actually thought about packing a bag and leaving for good. The whole thing is so awkward.

Chana: Why?

Olivia: Because. I messed everything up.

Chana: Is it true you messed everything up?

Olivia: Yes.

Chana: Can you absolutely know it's true?

Olivia: I think so.

Chana: And how do you react when you believe that?

Olivia: I get so nauseous, I want to throw up. And I feel like I can't breathe. That's why I left. As soon as I hit the street, I could breathe again. That always happens when things go wrong. It's not just that I messed up this one dinner, it's that I mess everything up. Let's get real: I'm broken.

Olivia has presented a challenge to me as a facilitator. On the one hand, Inquiry demands that we stick to one belief at a time and go through the entire process of questioning and re-evaluating it. Along the way, other thoughts pop up to say hello. When that happens, I usually write them down, adding them to my Thought Bank. In this case, I believe Olivia's uncovered a much more potent, pervasive, and pernicious belief. And I'd like to veer off course to address it. When facilitating others, this is an easier call to make, because I have an outsider's judgment. When I'm journaling on my own, I make a commitment to complete Inquiry on the thought at hand, lest I distract myself so much, I never get to the most meaningful part of Inquiry: the turnarounds.

Chana: You're broken, is that true?

Olivia: Of course it is!

Chana: Can you absolutely know it's true that you're broken?

Olivia: Yes. (Sobbing)

Chana: Why are you crying?

Olivia: Because it hurts so much. I hate being broken. It's like my insides are shattering.

Chana: What does your emotional reaction tell you about this belief?

Olivia: That it's the truest thing in the world. I'm not just broken, I feel broken! Look at me, I'm a buggery mess. I can't even hold it together!

Chana: Sounds to me like you're caught in The Bear Trap.

In the previous two chapters, we explored how our emotions and physiology serve as barometers. Our body is a Tuning Fork that lets us know when what we're believing serves us. Olivia's feeling horrible, so clearly, the idea that she's broken isn't working for her. If she were plugged into a Lie Detector, it would be raging, telling us that this belief is a lie.

Unfortunately, sometimes people get confused, thinking that if a thought makes them feel bad, it means it's *true*. It's a snare, a Bear Trap, catching us in confusion.

Chana: You've confused the brokenness of your emotional state with actually *being* broken.

Olivia: Well, what else am I supposed to think?

Chana: The real truth is embedded in your original thought. It's hiding in plain sight. Just say the opposite of it.

Olivia: You mean I'm supposed to believe I'm *not* broken?

Chana: Right now I'd simply like you to explore the thought. You've been stacking reasons why you're broken for years, right?

Olivia: Totally, I've got so many memories that pop up in my mind every time I think that thought.

Chana: In the same way, we're going to give supporting evidence for the belief that you're not broken and give it legs to stand on.

Olivia: Okay. So… I guess I'm good at being a seamstress. My customers are really happy with my work.

Chana: What else?

Olivia: Rob wanted to marry me, so there's got to be something good there.

Chana: And…

Olivia: Um… I'm stuck.

Chana: The brain is very literal. If you tell it you're broken, it gets all riled up because it believes you're literally broken, like a piece of wood that's been karate-chopped.

Olivia: Oh! In that case, I'm not broken. Not in that way. My body works just fine. I'm pretty fit, actually.

Chana: What else?

Olivia: I can see, and I've got good hearing. My toes are all in working order. I can read and talk and write.

Chana: Anything else?

Olivia: I know how to learn, so that's good. I guess I mess things up, but I can clean them up, too. Like the pot with the burnt tomato sauce. I gave it a good scrub, and it's as good as new. Still though…

Chana: What?

Olivia: I don't know. This belief feels like a deep part of me, like it's etched into my bones.

Chana: Is it *actually* etched into your bones?

Olivia: (Laughs) Okay. No. It's not. It just feels that way.

Chana: That just means you believe it strongly, that you've learned to identify with that belief, and have ingrained it by repeating it over the years.

Olivia: So I'm stuck with it?

Chana: No. Every time you state its opposite and live out your values, you reinforce new neural pathways. So let's explore another turnaround. What's another belief that opposes the idea that you're broken?

Olivia: I'm unbreakable.

Chana: How's that true?

Olivia: Well, I broke my leg doing gymnastics as a kid. It hurt and everything, but after a few months, it was totally healed. And I get cuts and scrapes that heal too.

Chana: How else is it true?

Olivia: (Laughs) This is embarrassing.

Chana: What is?

Olivia: Well, I finally came home after cooling off and my husband received me with this huge hug and we both apologized and it was fine. Better than fine, actually. Let's just say that dessert was way better than dinner!

Chana: Hmm...

Olivia: So my relationships can be healed even when I think they're irreparable. Apologies go a long way. I also think I'm unbreakable because at the end of the day I'm a soul. And souls live forever.

Chana: How does it feel to say that?

Olivia: Good, actually. I forget that most of the time. But my faith matters to me a lot, though when I'm believing I'm broken, I lose all faith. But believing I'm unbreakable connects me to G-d. He's unbreakable and I've got a part of Him in me. The most important part. Wow.

Chana: Wow, what?

Olivia: That's really big. Huge. I'm unbreakable.

Chana: How do you reconcile that with the botched dinner?

Olivia: Hmm... I don't know. Let me think about that.

Chana: Let's ask it this way: can something that's unbreakable create something broken?

Olivia: Oh. Yes, for sure. My pot is pretty solid, and it created a burnt sauce. And when I'm sewing, I have to be careful not to tear the fabric as it runs through the machine. The machine can stay strong even when the fabric is ruined.

Chana: What about you? What happens to you when the fabric tears?

Olivia: My body stays the same. My soul stays the same. But...

Chana: But what?

Olivia: I don't feel good about myself.

Chana: Is that because you're broken?

Olivia: Woah! No, it's not. It's because I *think* I'm broken. The thoughts come in and make me feel bad. But really, I'm the same person.

Chana: It just depends what story you decide to tell about the incident with the fabric.

Olivia: Yeah. When I was first learning to sew, I didn't feel bad when the fabric tore. My teacher made it seem like that's what happens to beginners. But now I feel like a loser when that happens. But only because I think I'm supposed to have it together. Like if I mess up, it means I'm broken, not just the fabric.

Chana: What do you want to do with this realization?

Olivia: I've got to write this down! I'm scared I'll forget.

Chana: Can you write it down in a way that's more memorable than some notes in your journal?

Olivia: (Bites lips) I could. I could do a needlepoint and hang it in my home.

Chana: What would it say?

Olivia: I've got something… What do you think of, "things can be broken, people can't?"

Chana: What do *you* think?

Olivia: I like it. I think it captures it all. I believed if I break things, make mistakes, it means something about me. But it doesn't. If I focus on the broken thing, I can try to fix it, like my broken leg. Or I can throw it away, like I should have done with the tomato sauce. But when I think it means *I'm broken,* I freeze up and get all upset. It's like I can't do anything useful. Woah.

Chana: What?

Olivia: The *thought* makes me *feel* broken. But I could imagine if I had the needlepoint close to my kitchen when I burnt the sauce, I could have just said, "things can be broken, people can't," and easily chucked the sauce into the trash and asked Rob to take me out for dinner. Instead, we both had to suffer through that nasty meal.

Chana: And the nasty conflict that ensued.

Olivia: Yuck.

Chana: What do you want to do?

Olivia: I want to go make my needlepoint. I know this thought is going to keep coming back, because I've said it in my mind so many times, but I can choose to think differently.

Chana: And every time you take an action that goes counter to the belief that you're broken, you weaken it in your brain.

Olivia: So it might stop coming back?

Chana: You'll know it's on its way out when you laugh at the thought of it.

Olivia: I like the sound of that!

Olivia was so entrenched in believing she was broken, it shaped her perception of her every action. Questioning her thinking expanded her understanding of what was possible. After giving solid support for empowering turnarounds, she came up with a way to remind herself of the strongest of them *every day.* Thoughts we believe are "written into our bones" usually got chiseled into us in early childhood. The best way to undo their damage is to travel back in time and help our younger selves undo the damage their confused minds have caused. For that, we need to step into The Time Machine, which we'll explore in the next chapter.

TUNING IN

Do you ever get caught in a Bear Trap by believing the intensity of your negative emotions is a reflection of the truth of your convictions? Think of one of those times and write down what you were believing that got you so riled up. Choose the belief most upsetting you and engage in Journal Inquiry with that belief, starting with Byron Katie's four questions and ending with as many turnarounds as you can come up with. Give support for each of these opposites and find tangible ways you can take action on them.

STRENGTHENING THE VOICE

But there are many other voices... pushing me to do everything possible to gain acceptance. They deny loudly that love is a totally free gift.

- Henri J.M. Nouwen

The Time Machine

The older you get, the more voices you get in the back of your head.

—Robert Jackson Bennett

Brandon couldn't figure out how to make his business profitable. He'd accumulated a slew of skills, know-how, and experience in the corporate world, but couldn't translate them into his own venture. In order to grow his business, he needed to market his products.

"But every time I think about creating ads, I freeze."

Since he believed investors were the ticket to success, Brandon was stuck. The problem is he couldn't be certain why he froze.

"Brandon," I said, "I'd like you to close your eyes and imagine a time you considered putting an ad together."

"I can already feel my body stiffening."

Brandon's energy was scattered, his mind was racing. He couldn't think straight. I decided to encourage him to do The Slow Poke.

"Slow time down. Identify the point when your body went from being calm to freezing."

"Okay. I'm there."

"It might seem like a micro-moment to you, but because your mind thinks in 10,000 words a minute, everything is happening at hyper-speed. To grasp the beliefs leading you to freeze, I'd like you to stretch that gap of time in your mind. Really slow it down."

As Brandon did so, I noticed his breathing become more regular.

Chana: There you go. What thoughts arise that cause your body to freeze?

Brandon: Salesmen are sleazy. I don't like dealing with money; money causes problems…

Chana: Is there more?

Brandon: I think a ton more, but those are the big ones.

Brandon was struggling with what I call a weak financial blueprint. Just like a contractor can look at an architect's blueprint and know what kind of structure will be built from it, we have blueprints of beliefs about different areas in our lives. Your financial blueprint is made up of what you believe (whether consciously or not) about money, wealthy people, work, and your ability to succeed or receive abundance. Shifting your financial blueprint is something my husband, Dave, and I cover in depth in our Money Mindset Challenge, which you can explore at MoneyMindsetMadness.com. For now, let's help Brandon overcome his money blocks.

In Brandon's case, we're already seeing that his money beliefs push him *away* rather than *towards* money. So it's no big surprise he's struggling. Because we develop most of our beliefs about money at an early age, I'm going to encourage Brandon to go into the Time Machine and identify a trigger for one of his beliefs.

Chana: Those three beliefs can massively hamper your success. Which one causes you to freeze the most?

Brandon: Money causes problems.

Chana: When was the earliest time you remember believing that money causes problems?

Brandon: I can see myself in the living room of my house growing up. My parents are fighting a ton. They're arguing about money.

Chana: How old are you?

Brandon: About seven or so.

Chana: We're going to give space for younger Brandon to do Inquiry and explore his beliefs. You'll be his mouthpiece and also share insights you've acquired as an adult.

Brandon: Alright.

Chana: Remember that my questions are directed towards him, not you. Brandon, how are you feeling?

Brandon: Sad. I don't like hearing my parents yell.

Chana: What else are you feeling?

Brandon: Scared.

Chana: What do those feelings make you want to do?

Brandon: I want to cry, I want to hide.

Chana: Do you?

Brandon: No. I just sit there frozen.

Chana: Feel anything else?

Brandon: Mad.

Chana: How mad?

Brandon: (whispers) Really, really mad.

Chana: What does that make you want to do?

Brandon: Hit someone. Yell. Yell, really, really loud.

Chana: Do you?

Brandon: No.

Brandon didn't know what to do with his emotions back when he was seven. He believed he had to swallow them; that they wouldn't be safe or accepted. When this happens, we not only trap the emotions in the body, we hold them inside a belief so we can access them later and, hopefully, release them in a healthy way when we do feel safe. The belief that money causes problems is a key to opening the door to Brandon's locked emotions.

Chana: Big Brandon, can you please walk into the scene and give little Brandon support? Ask him where he wants you to sit or stand and help him be comfortable feeling his sadness and anger.

Brandon: He wants me to sit next to him on the sofa and hold him.

We gave Brandon time to process these emotions and move them through his system. Finally, Brandon sighed and his breathing regulated, letting me know he was ready to continue.

Chana: Now, little Brandon, I want you to look at the situation again. Can you absolutely know it's true that money causes problems?

Brandon: I think so.

Chana: Can you absolutely *know* so?

Brandon: No.

Chana: What if we explored the opposite?

Brandon: Money doesn't cause problems?

Chana: Sure, that's one opposite. How might that be true?

Brandon: My parents didn't only fight about money.

Chana: There's one reason. Can you find another?

Brandon: It's just paper or coins. It can't really cause anything.

Chana: Insightful. What's another reason?

Brandon: My parents were fighting about how to spend the money they had, but if they didn't have any money, they might have been fighting about not having any.

Chana: So what were they fighting about?

Brandon: Hmmm.

Chana: Why did you say that?

Brandon: They were yelling about money, but they weren't playing tug-of-war with a wallet or anything!

Chana: That can lead us to the next turnaround. What can you replace the word "money" with in your original statement that money causes problems?

Brandon: Disagreements cause problems.

Chana: How's that true?

Brandon: Wow! I see it now! My parents were totally not on the same page! They argued about everything, how they spent their time, who they spent it with, how they parented us, you name it! Money is just one thing they fought about. But really, they were fighting about everything. They didn't match.

Chana: What else?

Brandon: They didn't trust each other. Especially when it came to money.

Chana: But was money at the root of the arguments?

Brandon: No. It wasn't.

Chana: So why do you think you chose to believe money was the problem?

Brandon: Good question. Why did I? I guess it meant I didn't have to blame my parents. It wasn't their fault they were fighting.

Chana: It was money's fault?

Brandon: Exactly.

Chana: But how does that leave you now?

Brandon: With parents who got divorced anyway and a fear of money.

Chana: So what do you want?

Brandon: I think I'd rather let my parents take the blame and feel more comfortable with money.

Chana: Big Brandon, if you chose to believe that, how does it affect the way you perceive the scene?

Brandon: I can see my parents are people struggling with themselves, with each other. But they're not imprisoned by money. So neither am I. (Smiles.)

Chana: Why did you smile?

Brandon: I'm not trapped. I can choose. I can decide how I want to relate to money. It doesn't control me.

Chana: What do you want to do?

Brandon: I want to build my business. I want to make money!

Chana: Why?

Brandon: Good question. Cause there's so much I want to do with it. I don't have to be scared it's going to hurt me.

Chana: This leads us to yet another turnaround, another opposite of money causes problems. Try reversing the word problems.

Brandon: Money causes solutions. I love that!

Chana: Why?

Brandon: Because it does. I can use it to buy food, pay rent, get clothing for my kids. I can use it to feed the homeless, to create technologies to make people's lives better. There's so many problems that can be solved with money. But...

Chana: But what?

Brandon: Well... not all problems can be solved with money. I mean, I don't think making more money would have saved my parents' marriage.

Chana: The belief we're exploring is "money causes problems," which we're questioning by looking at "money causes solutions," but the new statement doesn't say that it causes ALL solutions, right?

Brandon: Oh right! I can't go from thinking it's all bad to thinking it's a panacea. That's just as crazy. But I can see that it has the potential to be good if I choose to use it that way. And it can be the center of arguments if I want it to be.

Chana: Do you want it to be?

Brandon: No. I'd rather work on my communication with my wife and work out why each of us is upset and identify what's at the root.

Chana: How do you feel?

Brandon: More free, more open.

Chana: Close your eyes again. Reimagine that scene on the sofa when you were seven. How does it feel to revisit it?

Brandon: It's so much less charged. I feel calmer.

Trying to market his products triggered Brandon's money beliefs, but because they inhabited his subconscious, he didn't understand why he was freezing up. A journey in the Time Machine helped Brandon access the beliefs causing his upset. Once he knew what they were, we could tackle them one at a time through Inquiry.

THE TIME MACHINE IN A JOURNAL INQUIRY

We aim to make sense of the circumstance of our lives by making rules we believe will serve us and keep us safe. But, being human, we blunder.

Children are especially poor belief builders. A child might conclude his parents' divorce is his fault, though we as adults know quite the opposite is the case (many adults stay together because of their kids.) A child might conclude his mother ignores him because he's unlovable, though it's more likely Mom's preoccupied with stressors of her own. Brandon came to false conclusions about money to protect a pristine image of his parents.

Children (or adults in upsetting life events) create beliefs to make sense of their pain and confusion but often miss the opportunity to:

1.   Check the veracity of their assessments against the logic of a healthy adult.

2.   Share and process the emotional pain they're experiencing with a compassionate adult.

3.   Come to healthier conclusions that help them feel safer in the long run.

You, too, created rules and beliefs about life under times of stress. If you did that alone, you likely have some processing to do. You can now offer a more mature, conscious presence to that younger self. You can be the kindest, wisest, most compassionate friend to help the distressed soul you once were.

In your journal, do this by using two different colored pens (one for your current self, one for your younger self,) writing with opposing hands (e.g. right for current self, left for younger self,) or writing on different sides of the page.

The Time Machine is a portal for accessing the source of your current upset. I recommend you use The Time Machine when a gut sense tells you the belief you're dealing with is *old*. It's is also a key tool when a belief keeps nagging at you, even after you've addressed it through Inquiry.

As an example, I'll share a belief that nagged me for years.

My thought: There's something wrong with me.

It would come up every time I tripped, lost a friend, or got a bad grade. The circumstances that triggered my thought aren't its original source; they're simply pieces of evidence my mind's used to support a belief I created in the past. That's why new and unique events could just as easily trigger this belief to pop into my head.

To travel back in Time, ask yourself: **When was the earliest time I remember believing this thought?**

Try to answer this question from a more intuitive, rather than analytical, place. Allow an answer to bubble up to the surface. You might access a memory you've never recalled before or deemed significant. That's okay. Trust it.

In your journal, write the memory you've accessed. It helps if you can identify how old you were, where you were, who else was there, and what was happening. In my example, I recalled a memory of my father:

I'm sitting next to Papi in the den while he's watching a baseball game. I'm about 7. All of his attention is on the game. I want some of his attention. I also want to understand what's happening on the TV screen, because I don't know anything about baseball. I ask him a question and he tells me to be quiet.

Ask your younger self: **What emotions are you feeling during this memory?**

It's likely you're flooded with a mix of feelings. Focus on one emotion at a time. Write it in your journal, then close your eyes and give your body the time and space to feel it fully (it's likely you suppressed the emotion back then, which is why you've held onto this memory for so long.) Give yourself permission to cry, punch a pillow, scream, curse, etc. All emotion s are okay, acceptable, and safe. This is where you get to be the compassionate friend your past self really needed, one who is fully accepting. Don't rush this. Take your time. REMEMBER: Emotions are not thoughts! They're physical sensations easily identified in the body, not assessments of yourself and the world.

My emotions: sadness, anger, really furious rage, loneliness, despair

The original belief, "there's something wrong with me," has become an access point to a traumatic life event. My father ignoring me might not seem like "trauma" to you, but because the memory holds so many painful emotions and life defining beliefs, it is. These beliefs kept me trapped in unhealthy patterns for years. But by going into the past, I can access their root. I can help my younger self feel her emotions and identify and question her beliefs.

Ask your younger self The One Question: **What are you believing that's making you feel this way?**

Papi doesn't love me.

There's something wrong with me.

I'm doing something wrong.

I'm not lovable.

I hate baseball.

Baseball is stupid.

I hate Papi.

Papi hates me.

I'm not enough.

You might see much of yourself in the above list. It may be why you picked up this book. This list and the havoc it created inspired me to delve deep. I ended up learning the coaching tools that have transformed my mindset and helped my clients shift into more clarity, peace, and joy. The most potent transformations have happened in Journal Inquiries with my younger self.

It's important to stay actively involved in this conversation as a compassionate friend while giving full expression to your younger self.

Ask your younger self: **Which of these beliefs is the most upsetting?**

Note that, though my original belief is on the list, it might not be the most significant. Let's see what my younger self has to say.

> The thought I want to work on now: Papi doesn't love me.

Now it's time to facilitate Inquiry with your younger self. Again, I recommend you stick with *The Work* and use two different pens, opposing hands, or opposite sides of the page.

> 1. True? (Is it true?)
>
> Yes.
>
> 2. Absolutely? (Can you absolutely know that it's true?)
>
> Yes.
>
> 3. React? (How do you react when you believe the thought?)
>
> Cold, lonely. I close up. I want to cry. I want to roll up into an invisible ball. I want to punch Papi and yell at him.
>
> 4. Without? (How are you without the thought?)
>
> I can just enjoy his presence and be in the same room doing something I like more than watching baseball, like coloring or playing with my dolls. Or I can insist he give me attention without being attached to his response.

When my son was a toddler, he was so confident in himself, he assumed everyone was madly in love with him. So he'd insisted my father give him his undivided attention, and my father responded in kind. Sometimes that required him pulling my father down to the floor, plopping himself on his lap, or grabbing his face and forcing him to look into his eyes. When I watched him do this, I saw how much the world had responded to my insecurity, and how quickly I'd given up on people, including those who loved me the most, because my ego was so fragile. Amongst many things, this is why my son is my greatest teacher.

This leads us to our first (and most important) turnaround, the one that makes me the subject of my statement. I'll write it in my journal along with at least three reasons why it's true.

@ I don't love myself.

1. I take Papi's rejection personally.

2. I don't give myself the attention I want (maybe I could have hugged myself or talked kindly to myself at that moment.)

3. I thought mean things about me and Papi, which hurt me so much.

Because we're in The Time Machine, as far as our minds are concerned, we're *literally* in the past and can use our presence, wisdom, and love to heal that moment of brokenness. Noticing how I wasn't loving myself in that moment invites me to love myself in the present. I chose to imagine my adult self stepping into the scene.

Present Self (PS): How would you like to be loved right now?

Younger Self (YS): I want you to sit next to me.

PS: Anything else?

YS: (Nods.)

PS: What would you like?

YS: I want a hug.

I closed my eyes and imagined the both of us on that sofa, sitting together in a deep embrace. Both of us cried. Tears streamed down my face. I breathed all that love in. In and out. Giving it and receiving it - all to myself. It was a vulnerable thing to do, so courageous and full of heart. So nourishing.

PS: I love you soooooo much. Do you know that?

YS: (Shrugs.)

PS: Do you know why?

YS: No.

PS: Just because you are so deliciously lovable (notice I'm choosing to share a turnaround here.) But also because you're beautiful and special and curious and so so so good.

I committed to revisiting this young girl as many times as I could remember each day. Her cup needed a lot more filling up! I also decided to be more persistent in my relationship with my father by initiating more personal conversations, calling him frequently, and giving him tons of affection and appreciation every time he made an effort to connect. Our relationship massively shifted.

This turnaround taught me to be more loving and compassionate to myself. What did I learn from other turnarounds?

@ Papi does love me.

1. He works hard to put food on the table.

2. He takes me on trips.

3. He teaches me engineering stuff.

4. He invests in my education.

5. He buys me beautiful gifts.

6. He puts me on his shoulders in the pool.

It's so easy to push someone away because they don't meet our standards, but then we miss out on what they do have to offer. Even though my father didn't give me attention in that moment, he was there for me so many other times. My mind just chose to hyper-focus on the memory of being in the den and downplayed everything else about him. It was an unfair, skewed representation of reality, and it hurt.

I'd like to explore one last turnaround, one that called me to step outside of my little bubble of pain and hold space for my father's experience.

@ Papi doesn't love himself.

1. He's stressed and wants to watch TV to avoid feeling that pain, even though it's not as nourishing as spending time with someone he loves.

2. He's missing out on connecting with a great kid.

3. He's craving love and affection, but won't let it in, even when it's presented to him on a silver platter.

I shared this memory with my father a couple years after this Journal Inquiry. He told me it pained him, but that he didn't want to live in a regretful past. He'd rather be in a loving present with me now, which he really is! We laugh together, text loving notes, and talk on the phone often. My work created an opening for our relationship to deepen, and Papi accepted the invitation with courage, compassion, and love. I'm crying just writing this. It's been the most healing work I've ever done. And the reason this book is dedicated to him.

Papi, if you're reading this, I love you. Thank you for showing up for me in so many ways, big and small. And thank you for being patient in letting me grow up enough to see that.

TUNING IN

You've always wanted to time travel, haven't you? Here's your chance! Dive into The Time Machine. Be prepared to dedicate at least 30 uninterrupted minutes to this work. The Time Machine demands your full attention, presence, and compassion, so use this tool when you're capable of giving them to yourself.

Look through your Thought Banks and select a belief you sense is rooted in the past. Ask yourself, "When was the earliest time I remember believing that thought?" Then facilitate your younger self through a paced and attentive Inquiry. If you believe you're hitting material more potent than you can manage on your own, please reach out to book a session with me or someone on my team.

Remember to offer your younger self the space and kindness they need to learn and heal from the challenges of the past.

Missing the Target

If we have no quiet,
we will hear plenty of noise,
but we will not hear a single voice.

—Craig D. Lounsbrough

About a month after my fifth birthday, my sisters and I were in our living room having a guitar lesson when we heard a knock at the door. Our housekeeper innocently opened it, not realizing there were five armed men on the other side. They quickly stormed their way into our home and put a gun to my mother's head. After forcing her to open her safe and finding it empty, they planted the gun at her temple in hopes they could embezzle money out of us, even threatening to kidnap my sisters and me. Mami didn't consider this an empty threat. This was 1983 in Bogota, Colombia. We knew people who'd lost family members to kidnapping.

Eventually, my mother used her charm to convince them she'd get cash together by the next day. Somehow, they believed her and left us shaking and traumatized. My parents upended their lives and, within a couple days, we fled the country and moved to Miami.

I've spent many a therapy session processing this experience. Like an onion, it's held layers of pain, fear, and confusion, which I unpacked at a pace my psyche and body felt safe to explore. This is a pattern for many of us. We revisit the most life-altering events repeatedly until they can finally rest.

I recently told my coach I thought childhood trauma was triggering a persistent stream of migraine headaches, but couldn't access anything. I thought perhaps I should explore hypnosis. She asked me a surprising question: "What do you want to find?"

My mouth spoke before I could even process her question. "I think something from when we fled Colombia."

Immediately, an image popped into my mind. I saw my hands outstretched towards my childhood home, my nails gripping it for dear life. And someone was dragging me away.

Tears flooded my eyes.

My coach recommended I sit with that memory with compassion and understanding. And so I did.

That night, after I showered, I sat wrapped in a warm blanket and closed my eyes. I sank into meditative breathing.

And BOOM.

The memory came alive.

I was screaming "NO!" Every ounce of my being was screaming "NO!"

I'd been ripped away from my home, my life, my language, everything I knew. And I DID NOT ALLOW it.

I was trapped in the ultimate challenge of life. Reality was playing itself out, and I was fighting it. Tooth and nail.

Byron Katie says when we fight with reality, we always lose. Reality's going to do what it's going to do. That includes war, rape, murder, death, disease, tooth decay, bounced checks, lousy restaurants, spouses who cheat. These are, for reasons beyond our understanding, inevitable parts of the human experience.

We can be at war with life, or we can accept it. That's the choice.

And that little five-year-old girl was *not* accepting it. She was raging against what she perceived to be the dying of the light.

Between tears, I attempted to put this visceral war into words. This is the Thought Bank I created:

The bad men shouldn't have barged into our home.

They were wrong.

It was all wrong.

My parents should have protected me.

They shouldn't have taken me away from my home.

They should have asked my permission to go to Miami.

The world is not a safe place.

I will never be safe again.

I can never forgive them.

The belief that most caught my attention, the one that upset me the most was, "The world is not a safe place." (Ironically, or appropriately, this is a belief many of my clients struggle with as well.) I decided to facilitate my younger self through Inquiry and see if we could ease the panic that was rushing through my limbs.

Chana: Is it true that the world isn't a safe place?

Young Me (YM): Yes.

Chana: Can you absolutely know it's true?

YM: Yes. Definitely. I was almost kidnapped!

Chana: How do you react when you believe that the world isn't safe?

YM: I want to curl up. I feel very small.

Chana: Anything else?

YM: I look around myself, searching for danger. I can't settle down.

Chana: Do any emotions come up?

YM: I feel scared. And sad. And shaky. And I keep picturing all these bad things happening.

Chana: Okay. Take a deep breath. Be there in Colombia, in that moment. And imagine yourself without the thought that the world is not a safe place.

YM: I don't think I can.

Chana: Okay. Keep breathing slowly. Imagine that thought stepping out of your body and becoming a creature.

YM: Okay. I can do that.

Chana: What do you see?

YM: A big hairy gorilla.

Chana: What does it like to eat?

YM: Chips and Candy. (Laughs)

Chana: Why'd you laugh?

YM: Because I thought it was going to say it wanted to eat me, but it just liked my favorite junk food.

Chana: (Laughs) Great. So let's go with that. Can you give the gorilla a big wad of cash and send him off to the supermarket to buy as much candy and chips as he wants?

YM: Yeah. He's all excited.

Chana: Perfect. So there you are without the gorilla and his words that the world is not a safe place.

YM: I'm still scared.

Chana: Why?

YM: Because of the men. The men are scary.

Chana: I see. And how were you before the men walked in the door?

YM: I was fine. I was playing guitar. I like music.

Chana: Did you feel safe then?

YM: I guess so. Yes, actually. I couldn't play music if I wasn't safe. As soon as the men stormed into the house, I dropped my guitar. I couldn't think of anything but those men.

Chana: So were you wrong about the world being safe when you were playing guitar?

YM: Hm…. Maybe I was just stupid.

Chana: Do you believe that?

YM: Now that I think about it, no. I was safe when I was playing guitar. But the bad men weren't safe.

Chana: Does that mean the world isn't safe?

YM: Wait a second.

Chana: What?

YM: When I believe the world isn't safe, it's like EVERYTHING is scary and dangerous. But that's not true. Only some things are. Only some people are.

Chana: So what's more true?

YM: That some people or places aren't safe. But…

Chana: But what?

YM: But then I'm not on guard.

Chana: What do you mean?

YM: Well, when I believe the world isn't safe, I can protect myself better. From bad people like the men.

Chana: So, just to clarify, you think if you believe the world is not a safe place, you'll be safer?

YM: Yes. Exactly.

At that moment, I popped out of Inquiry for a minute, just long enough to laugh long and hard. Why? Because I sounded like so many of my clients. They also Miss the Target.

What do I mean by that?

We believe what we do because we expect our beliefs will lead us towards the things we want: happiness, health, safety, love….

But often, our beliefs drive us in exactly the opposite direction.

As I was laughing, I was thinking about Darnell, a character in the book *The Size of Your Dreams* I co-wrote with my husband, Dave. Darnell is obese and wants to lose weight. So, he espouses the belief he "should lose weight" in the hopes it will lead him towards healthier habits.

Why don't you try that belief on for size? Imagine yourself in front of a buffet table covered in your favorite treats. While you're picturing this table, soak in the belief that you should lose weight. How does the belief make you feel? What does it make you want to do?

The hundreds of students, clients, and workshop participants I've surveyed say that believing they should lose weight makes them want to dive towards the table and devour everything in sight. They want to eat *more*, not less.

Darnell realized this belief was blocking him from achieving the very goal he set out for himself. And in thinking about him, I realized that believing the world wasn't a safe place was making even the safest of moments in my daily life *feel* dangerous. It wired up my nervous system and made me hide from life. My younger self hoped this belief would lead me to safety and happiness, but it only led to misery. I now questioned whether it was helping me protect myself.

Chana: Let's test this theory of yours that this belief helps you be safer.

YM: What do you mean?

Chana: What happens to your vision when you believe the world is not a safe place?

YM: It gets kind of blurry.

Chana: And what about at the edges?

YM: The edges are blocked off. I can't see anything there.

Chana: How well does your mind work when you're believing this thought?

YM: I'm really focused on danger. It feels tight. And muddled with a ton of thoughts.

Chana: Not so creative?

YM: No. Not at all.

Chana: How about your muscles?

YM: They're all tight. And my body gets really small. Like I said before. I just want to curl up.

Chana: What about your stomach?

YM: That feels tight too. And I'm kind of nauseous.

Chana: Now let's look at everything you've said. Your vision gets blurry, you can't see at the edges at all, your mind is racing, your creativity is zero, your muscles are tight and your body gets small. And oh yeah, you're nauseous.

YM: Right.

Chana: Do you think being this way makes you more or less capable of dealing with danger?

YM: Oh. I get it. Much much less. I'm kind of useless in that state.

Chana: Yep. So is this belief getting you where you want to go?

YM: I guess not.

Chana: What do you actually want?

YM: I want to feel cozy and calm and happy. I want to be creative and flexible and playful and fun, which is really how I am when I'm not scared.

Chana: Working backward, what belief would give you that experience?

YM: I'm like that when I feel safe. So I guess when I believe I am safe.

Chana: That brings us to your first turnaround.

YM: The world is a safe place?

Chana: Yes. How's that true?

YM: I have food. More than I need, even.

Chana: What else?

YM: I have a family that takes care of me. I have a place to live. Even in Miami, we easily found a place to live.

Chana: Since this is a strong belief, let's list out lots and lots of reasons.

YM: My body is healthy. And when I get sick, my parents and the doctor take care of me. Most of the people I meet are helpful. My teachers are helpful and the people at the store. I have a big extended family who care about me. I have a toilet and running water and soap. All these things keep me safe.

Chana: Because I'm you. And I've been you for many many more years, I can add all sorts of things you don't know about.

YM: Like what?

Chana: I've lived over four decades and I'm still here. Healthy, physically strong, living the life of my dreams.

YM: But you live in Israel.

Chana: And the vast majority of the people here are kind and helpful and care about my safety. There's little crime here. And as we sit here together, wrapped up in this blanket, we're perfectly safe. We're okay.

YM: But maybe one day something will happen, you could get hurt.

Chana: Perhaps. But perhaps not. That's the thing about doing Inquiry. It's not about absolutes. It's just a matter of recognizing that "the world is a safe place" is *more true* than "the world is not a safe place." And the question is, which do I prefer to believe? Which one makes me feel better and more accurately represents reality?

YM: Most of the time, we're safe.

Chana: Exactly. Until that day the men came into your house—and that only happened for a few hours—you were just fine.

YM: (smiles) Yes. I was.

Chana: Why did you smile?

YM: I didn't think it was okay to pay attention to that. I thought I had to hold on to that moment when the men came in.

Chana: When you believed the world wasn't safe, you had to. You could only focus on the unsafe parts. And because there haven't been that many of them, you had to blow this one up real big.

YM: I still don't like that we left Colombia. It was home.

Chana: So let's work on that next. For now, do you feel done with this thought?

YM: Yes. It's okay to relax and let go. It's okay to believe the world is safe. It feels good.

I closed my eyes and let these new thoughts settle. I soaked in the softness of my blanket as I imagined hugging my younger self and giving her my protection, love, and comfort. I could be a source of safety for myself. I realized the world is a safe place because I'm a resourceful and capable person. I can take care of myself. I know how to identify dangerous people and situations. And I can do that more easily when I'm calm and in touch with myself and not on edge and erratic.

As many children do, my younger self had Missed the Target in her assessment of which beliefs would lead to her desired outcomes. Identifying the junky outcomes she actually got pushed her to embrace new perspectives.

TUNING IN

It's time for target practice! Every belief is like a hammer. The question is, what's the nail? What is this belief designed to make happen? Take one of the beliefs from your Thought Banks and ask yourself the following questions:

1. What am I hoping to achieve by believing this thought?

2. What outcomes do I *actually* get from believing this thought?

3. What beliefs would help me achieve my desired outcomes more effectively?

4. How can I actualize those beliefs in my life starting now?

Resourse Replay

The human being is very resourceful. When you fight for survival, you don't think much; you just do. If you think too much, you sink.

—Frank Lowy

S ophia loved her work as a copywriter but struggled to make ends meet financially. She didn't want to leave her job but felt trapped by her circumstances.

Sophia: They really should pay me more.

Chana: Why do you believe that?

Sophia: Because I'm still getting the same salary I had when I first started with the magazine five years ago. But I was right out of college then. Now I have real experience.

Chana: Why do you believe that means they should pay you more?

Sophia: Because it just makes sense. I'm worth more. It's what I would get paid if I applied for a job elsewhere.

Chana: Are you applying for a job elsewhere?

Sophia: No. I don't want to leave. I like the people at the magazine, and it's comfortable there. It's like a second home to me.

Chana: Do your superiors know that?

Sophia: I think so. They know I've made friends at the magazine. And I'm there all the time, even having drinks with the crew after hours.

Chana: Why do you believe you're not getting paid more?

Sophia: I don't know. Maybe they don't think I'm so good? Or they don't believe in me?

Chana: What reason did they give you?

Sophia: What do you mean?

Chana: What did they say when you asked for a raise?

Sophia: Oh. I didn't. That would be so uncomfortable.

Chana: Why?

Sophia: Because I don't want to impose. It's so awkward. I'm squirming just thinking about it. What if they say no?

Chana: What's your answer to that question?

Sophia: I'd be crushed. I couldn't handle it. It would be so embarrassing going back into the office. I'd never be able to look them in the eye again.

Chana: Why?

Sophia: Because then it would be out there.

Chana: What would be?

Sophia: That I'm really not so good. That they only have me there cause I'm entry-level quality and cheap labor, essentially.

Chana: Earlier you said it makes sense for you to get paid more, that you've got experience, that you'd be offered a higher salary elsewhere.

Sophia: Yeah, but…

Chana: But what?

Sophia: Deep inside I'm scared that's not true. It's what my friends tell me to make me feel better, but I can't rely on that.

As I spoke with Sophia, I took notes on the beliefs she said outright or implied and build the following Thought Bank:

Sophia's Words	My Thought Bank
They really should be paying me more.	They should be paying me more..
Because I'm still getting the same salary I had when I first started with the magazine five years ago. But I was right out of college then. Now I have real experience.	I should get paid more because now I have real experience.
Because it just makes sense. I'm worth more. It's what I would get paid if I applied for a job elsewhere.	I should get paid more because it makes sense. I should get paid more because I'm worth more. I should get paid more because it's what I would get elsewhere. They should know I want to get paid more.
I don't want to leave. I like the people at the magazine, and it's comfortable there. It's like a second home to me.	I don't want to leave. I like the people at the magazine. It's comfortable there. It's like a second home to me.
I think [they know I don't want to leave.] They know my closest friends are at the magazine. And I'm there all the time, even having drinks with the crew after hours.	They know I don't want to leave. They know my closest friends are at the magazine. I'm there all the time.
I don't know [why they're not paying me more.] Maybe they don't think I'm so good? Or they don't believe in me?	I don't know why I'm not getting paid more. They don't think I'm so good. They don't believe in me.
I didn't [ask for a raise]. That would be so uncomfortable.	It would be uncomfortable to ask for a raise.

Sophia's Words	My Thought Bank
Because I don't want to impose. It's so awkward. I'm squirming just thinking about it. What if they say no? I'd be crushed. I couldn't handle it. It would be so embarrassing going back into the office. I'd never be able to look them in the eye again.	I don't want to impose. It's awkward to ask for a raise. If they say no, I'd be crushed. If they say no, I couldn't handle it. If they say no, it would be embarrassing going back into the office. If they say no, I'd never be able to look them in the eye again.
Because then it would be out there. That I'm really not so good. That they only have me there cause I'm entry-level quality and cheap labor, essentially.	I'm really not so good. They only have me there cause I'm entry-level quality and cheap labor.
Deep inside I'm scared that's not true. It's what my friends tell me to make me feel better, but I can't rely on that.	It's not true that I've got experience, and would be offered a higher salary elsewhere My friends tell me these things to make me feel better. I can't rely on what my friends say.

If just reading this Thought Bank brings you down, imagine what believing all these thoughts has been doing to Sophia. Of course she feels trapped. No matter what she does, she feels bad. If she asks for what she wants, she exposes herself to massive rejection. And if she doesn't, she's strapped for cash, and her self-worth is in the gutter. I read the list to Sophia and asked her to pick the belief that felt the most true and simultaneously the most gut-wrenching.

Sophia: If they say no, I couldn't handle it. That one feels like it encompasses a lot. I think I've always believed that one.

Chana: How so?

Sophia: I remember being at school and struggling with something, but not raising my hand to ask a question.

Chana: You were scared the teacher wouldn't answer your question?

Sophia: It was more like being scared she'd see how dumb I was or that other kids would laugh at me. It was better to hide.

Sophia's already pointing to an episode in her past. I took this as an invitation to jump into the Time Machine.

Chana: If it's alright with you, I'd like to take you back there. Perhaps if you can help your younger self reconcile with her fears, she can help you with your own.

Sophia: Alright.

Chana: Close your eyes and imagine one of those times you're struggling in school. How old are you? What's the topic challenging you?

Sophia: I'm in grade three, I think. We're learning fractions, and I just can't seem to get it.

Chana: You can see little Sophia there in the classroom?

Sophia: Yes. She's sharing a table with another girl, Irene. Irene is super smart.

Chana: Ask little Sophia if she'd like you, as an adult, to step into the scene. And if so, where would she like you to be?

Sophia: She wants me to pull up a chair and sit right next to her.

Chana: Great. Now give her a remote control she can use to shift the scene. For now, ask her to press pause, so you and she can talk freely without the other kids noticing.

Sophia: Okay.

Chana: What is she feeling?

Sophia: She's scared. Her heart's racing. She doesn't want people to think she's stupid. She's scared if people really see her, they won't like her.

Chana: That's a lot for a little girl to feel. And she swallowed those emotions, trapping them deep down until now. Can you give her the space to feel those emotions?

Sophia: Ugh. It feels horrible.

Chana: If you give them permission to be felt, they'll move through you quite quickly, otherwise she'll be stuck in that fear and trauma indefinitely.

In this dialogue, in addition to straight Inquiry, I also guided Sophia through a modified version of Brendon Bays' *The Journey.* Sophia permitted herself to fully feel her fear, and when I saw a shift in her disposition, I dug deeper.

Chana: Is there an emotion under the fear?

Sophia: She's sad. It's lonely not being able to speak up.

Chana: She's held onto that sadness so tightly for so many years. Allow it to move through your body. There. It's okay to cry. I see you.

Sophia: Poor thing. I didn't realize how lonely it was. I guess it's still lonely holding myself back so much.

Chana: Is there another emotion under the sadness?

Sophia: Anger. Wow. A lot of anger. I think at my mom. She was always so composed. So… Parisian. Never a hair out of place. I think she wanted me to be a showpiece, part of her perfect wardrobe.

Chana: Notice all of that, without attaching to the thoughts. Just notice the anger. Little Sophia, is there anything you want to do with all that rage?

Sophia: I want to punch my desk.

Chana: So do that!

Sophia: And I want to punch the teacher. Is that okay?

Chana: Yes. Go ahead.

Sophia: Amazing. That actually feels so much better. I can breathe more freely now.

Chana: Why don't you invite your mother into the scene in the classroom. Is there anything you want to say to her?

Sophia: What if she gets mad at me?

Chana: Little Sophia, in this space, it's safe to say what you feel. She'll hear you.

Sophia: Alright. *Maman,* I'm not a doll. I don't know what I'm doing and I want help. And I don't want to be scared to ask for help. And I want you to see when I'm hurting or scared or confused and help me.

Chana: How does it feel to say that?

Sophia: (Wipes tears from face.) Good. You're right. She's hearing me. And she's so sad because she didn't intend to hurt me. She thinks I'm wonderful just the way I am. She says she's sorry and she hugs me.

Chana: How does that feel?

Sophia: So comforting.

Chana: Be with that. Breathe it in. Soak in her love and her words.

Sophia: (Smiles)

Sophia's childhood beliefs depleted her, leaving her feeling incapable of dealing with life's challenges. To battle this disempowerment, I invited Sophia to access the Resources, the emotional strengths, lying dormant inside her. Through Resource Replay, she'll be able to tap into these Resources whenever she wants to and be her own hero.

Chana: Now both of you together, look at this scene in the classroom and consider what emotional Resources would have helped Little Sophia navigate the experience better and get what she wanted.

Sophia: Courage would have been good, without fear of what others would think.

Chana: What else?

Sophia: Self-confidence, strength. And love. I can see all my mother's love makes me feel better. If I had been aware of it then, I wouldn't have been so scared.

Chana: Any other Resources?

Sophia: No. I think these are good.

Chana: Now I'd like you, Big Sophia, to think of something that Little Sophia would love to get as a gift. Perhaps a toy or a book.

Sophia: She was always obsessed with her stuffed bears and couldn't get enough of them.

Chana: Keep your eyes closed. And now, Big Sophia, imagine you have a collection of fluffy new bears next to you. Each one embodies one of the Resources you've listed. Take the first of these, the Bear of Courage, and give it to Little Sophia. Little Sophia, I want you to imagine this bear radiating courage. Hug that bear and feel all that light seep into your heart and then travel to every part of you, from the top of your head to the tips of your toes, filling you up with courage. And when you've done so, and you're ready, imagine that bear shrinking to the size of a marble, so you can put it in your pocket for safe-keeping.

In a slow and present way, Sophia proceeded to gift her younger self with the Bears of Self-Confidence, Strength, and Love. As she did so, her breathing grew deeper, her posture rose, and her general disposition eased into a calm joy. In other words, her Tuning Fork was ringing true.

Chana: Now, Sophia, it's time for Resource Replay. Think of all the times in your life that feel like this scene, where you believed you wouldn't be able to handle a "no."

Sophia: There are so many of those!

Chana: That's fine. Imagine them all playing out in sequence, one after the other, like in a fast-paced movie reel, only this time, picture yourself in each of these scenes full of your Resources: Courage, Self-Confidence, Strength, and Love.

Sophia: Oh. That's so different. I'm a different person in those scenes. I stand tall and have a voice. I can handle a "no." Definitely.

Sophia has come to the first turnaround on her own. Her original belief was "If they say no, I couldn't handle it." Here, she's already seeing herself "handling it." To reinforce this understanding, we'll return to Inquiry and give her the opportunity to offer up supporting evidence.

Chana: How do you know you can handle it?

Sophia: I'm okay no matter what people say. I can see that I've gotten plenty of "no's" either because I asked or because not asking also gave me a "no," and I was totally fine.

Chana: How else?

Sophia: Because the teacher might've said no, but she wouldn't have beat me. Even if the other kids laughed, which happened sometimes, I still went back to school and was okay. And also because my parents love me. When I'm full of love, I know that. But in that classroom, I thought I was all alone and not loved, but it wasn't true.

Chana: Now let's fast forward to the present day. Imagine yourself filled with these Resources at the office. As you think about your desire for a higher salary, picture yourself infused with Courage, Self-Confidence, Strength, and Love.

Sophia: It feels amazing. I feel more connected to my colleagues. It's obvious now that I'm an integral part of the team.

Chana: Now why do you believe they're not paying you more?

Sophia: (Laughs)

Chana: Why'd you laugh?

Sophia: Why should they? The way I've behaved, they can assume I don't care. The magazine industry is tight. If they can get someone like me for cheap, it's a great deal for them. But if I ask for more, they know it would be risky for them to say no.

Chana: Why?

Sophia: Because they'd lose me.

Chana: I thought you said you wouldn't leave.

Sophia: I love it there, but with all this strength in me, I'm not going to put up with crappy pay. I'd have the confidence to walk out and get a better position elsewhere. I could make new friends at another magazine.

Chana: Do you still believe if they said, "no," you couldn't handle it?

Sophia: No way! (Laughs) I'd be fine. I'd retort with reasons why they should pay me more and thus keep me. And if they don't want to, then I'd go look for a better gig.

Chana: How does it feel to say that?

Sophia: So liberating! I don't feel trapped anymore.

Chana: How do you want to remind yourself of the Resources?

Sophia: I like the idea of getting myself bears. Little silver ones I could put in a charm bracelet. Just the idea makes me feel strong!

Sophia didn't feel resourceful enough to ask for what she wanted. Traveling back to an early memory allowed her to tap into an early source of the beliefs she was presently struggling with. By helping Little Sophia heal her fear and confusion, she was open to accessing the vast wealth of Resources inside of herself. By engaging in Resource Replay, she found the fortitude to combat the destructive beliefs holding her back.

TUNING IN

Think of a time you felt incapable of getting your needs met or of dealing with the challenges of life. Ask yourself The One Question to access the beliefs holding you back. Then step into The Time Machine to step into the earliest memory during which you were believing a similar collection of thoughts. Once you've given your younger self a chance to emotionally and verbally express his/her layers of upset, ask yourself what Resources would have helped you navigate that moment more effectively. Write them down and then imagine yourself gifting your younger self those Resources through a bear, a book, or some other trinket.

Imagine each trinket radiating its Resource into your younger self. Have your younger self hug that trinket and feel the Resource seep into their heart and infuse every part of them, from the top of their head to the tips of their toes. When they've done so, imagine that trinket shrinking to the size of a marble, so they can put it in their pocket for safe-keeping.

Once they've suffused your being with those Resources, Replay every scene in your life that was similar to this one; only this time, imagine yourself fully Resourceful. How are these scenes different? What do you believe now? Write down your new understandings and reflections. Then find daily strategies for keeping those Resources active in your life.

To learn more about **Resource Replay,**
access **Free Bonus Materials** at
ChanaMason.com/Inner-Voices-Bonus.

Guideposts

"We are shaped by our thoughts; we become what we think. When the mind is pure, joy follows like a shadow that never leaves.

—Buddha

J ason's nails were bitten down to the skin, and he was picking at his cuticles.

Chana: What has you so anxious?

Jason: My brother, Billy. He's depressed. He texted me saying he was going to kill himself. It's like the hundredth time he's done that. It's so stressful.

Chana: What about that upsets you?

Jason: Isn't it obvious? Wouldn't you be upset if you got a message like that?

Chana: If I got that message, I might be upset, but my reasons might not be the same as yours. What's important is why *you're* upset.

Jason: It's frustrating. I have to put my whole life on hold every time he does that. It's constant crisis intervention. (Shakes head.)

Chana: Why'd you just shake your head?

Jason: Things aren't working for Billy, but he's not doing anything to make his life better. He should change what he's doing.

We can already see the beginnings of a Thought Bank.

My Thought Bank
He's depressed.
He's going to kill himself.
It's so stressful.
I should be upset when I get a suicide message from my brother.
I have to put my whole life on hold every time he does that.
It's constant crisis intervention.
Things aren't working for him.
He's not doing anything to make his life better.
He should change what he's doing.

I read Jason what I'd written and asked him which of the beliefs was the most upsetting.

Jason: I get riled up when I think about how stuck he is. So I would say that he should change what he's doing.

Chana: Okay. Close your eyes and picture yourself in that moment when you got Billy's text. Is it true that he should change what he's doing?

Jason: YES! Damn it! YES! (Punches fist into the arm of his chair.)

Chana: Why'd you just punch your fist like that?

Jason: Because I'm so mad! I'm really frustrated with him. He should really get his stuff together, you know?

Chana: The belief makes you really mad. With what we've learned about the Lie Detector, what does that tell you?

Jason: I guess you want me to say the tension and anger mean the belief isn't true.

Chana: What *I want* you to say?

Jason: Yeah. But I don't buy it. I mean, there's so much energy here. It's gotta mean this thought is true.

Chana: Why do you believe that?

Jason: Because I'm *feeling so much*. That's gotta mean something. It's gotta mean what I'm believing is really important.

In a way, Jason was caught in the Bear Trap. He assumed the fire of his emotions was a reflection of the veracity of his belief. It became clear over the course of our conversation that his anger and frustration were actually pointing to something else entirely.

Chana: You're feeling quite intensely. And I agree it's a sign this belief is important. But does important necessarily mean *true*?

Jason: What else am I supposed to do? Think Billy's fine the way he is and ignore him?

Chana: Is that really your only other option?

Jason: Umm… I don't know.

Chana: Not knowing is a great place to start. From not knowing we can begin to question our thinking.

Jason: Okay. I hear that. I just don't know how to let him go, how to let him take himself on such a downward spiral.

Chana: Does your believing he should change *actually* change him?

Jason: Well, it gets me to help him out sometimes.

Chana: And does that *change* Billy?

Jason: It makes his apartment cleaner. For a little while. But… oh… wait…

Chana: What?

Jason: Maybe when I go over and clean his apartment, I'm making him feel even more useless. It's like I'm telling him he's not capable on his own.

Chana: How do you feel about that?

Jason: Disappointed. I can see… it's like I don't respect him. I can't imagine that makes it so easy for him to respect himself.

Chana: So is this anger serving you?

Jason: Oh. I get it. All that emotion I felt from the belief. I was thinking it was helping push me. I guess it did push me. To barrel into Billy...

Chana: Are you ready to question this belief that's causing you to do that?

Jason: Yes.

Chana: Great. Now close your eyes again and picture yourself in that moment when you got the text from your brother. Is it true he should change what he's doing?

Jason: I still believe it's true. But I'm no longer going to attack the furniture.

Chana: Good to hear. Let's dig a little deeper. Can you absolutely know it's true he should change what he's doing?

Jason: No.

Chana: We know how you react when you believe the thought, so let's leap right to what's driving the rush of emotions you're feeling.

Jason: What do you mean?

Chana: Our emotions let us know if what we're believing is in alignment with truth, with reality. But they also point us in the direction we want to go. If the emotions are open and uplifting they encourage us to keep moving forward. But if we're feeling closed, tight, upset, then we're being guided to change course.

Jason: So how do I know what course to take?

Chana: The answers are all embedded in the turnarounds. What's the opposite of 'he should change what he's doing?'

Jason: He shouldn't change what he's doing.

Chana: How's that true?

Jason: He doesn't feel excited to change. He thinks life is hopeless.

Chana: What else?

Jason: Um... I don't know. This is hard.

Chana: What happens when he tells you he's depressed and suicidal?

Jason: I check in on him multiple times a day. We all do, my parents, my sister, my cousins. It's a whole family affair.

Chana: Seems like it's serving him.

Jason: I never thought of it that way, but yeah. He gets to be the center of attention. It's just a crappy way to get attention. Man... He shouldn't be doing that.

Chana: Do you have any control over how he chooses to get attention?

Jason: No. But... but wait. I kind of do. I can choose to ignore him when he's like this and give him more attention when he's doing things to make his life better. I can talk to him differently.

Chana: Can you guarantee that'll work to change his strategy?

Jason: Not really... But maybe that's okay. At least *I* can be saner. I don't have to be caught in a vortex.

Chana: This brings us to another turnaround. Why don't you make yourself the subject?

Jason: I should change what *I'm* doing?

Chana: Can you give me some reasons why that's true?

Jason: Yeah. I should change how I treat him. We all coddle him and treat him like the baby of the family cause he's the youngest. But man, he's in his fifties. Not exactly a baby. And I can ask him what he's planning on doing to make things better rather than telling him what to do.

Chana: One thing powerful about turnarounds is how they serve as Guideposts, reminding us of our values and clarifying what's important to us. You've looked at how you can change what you're doing in regards to the way you treat your brother. What values do you think are embedded in this turnaround?

Jason: Something about personal responsibility. Like he's his own person, you know? Perhaps the word is independence. Also respect, both for me and for him. And also listening. I could listen to him better rather than just worry and try to shove my strategies onto him.

Chana: That also seems more humble of you. Perhaps you don't have all the answers.

Jason: Yeah. I like that. Humility. I know I'm no hot-shot, but I often act that way around Billy.

Chana: Now let's look at that turnaround again. When you believed Billy should change, I assume you had a list in your mind of all the ways he should change.

Jason: For sure.

Chana: What's on your list?

Jason: He should exercise, eat healthier, socialize, sleep during normal hours, go to church.

Chana: Anything else?

Jason: Hmm…. Oh, Yes. This is a big one. He should stretch himself professionally by working harder, taking risks, or trying for a better job.

Both of these turnarounds shine a spotlight on a number of Billy's values.

Jason's Turnarounds	Jason's Values
He shouldn't change what he's doing.	Personal responsibility, respect, independence, autonomy, humility.
I should change what I'm doing.	Exercise, healthy eating, sleep, spiritual life, community, taking risks, hard work

But Guideposts only work if we take their direction. Activating our desire to live in alignment with our values by taking actionable steps is what leads us on the path towards integrity

Chana: Let's take a look at that list for guidance as to how you should change.

Jason: (Laughs)

Chana: Why'd you laugh?

Jason: That's a mighty tall order!

Chana: You didn't seem to think so when it came to Billy.

Jason: Good point.

Chana: So look at this list of shoulds and turn them around to be about Jason.

Jason: Okay. I should exercise. That's true. I keep gaining a little more weight every winter and not shedding it in the summer, so my gut's looking like Dad's. And he's diabetic. Not a great recipe. I guess that goes with eating healthier. I could improve there too.

Chana: What about sleep?

Jason: The thing is… I don't know, I have my kids and work and…

Chana: And what?

Jason: Those are just excuses. I've got a ton of excuses about food and exercise, too. But really, I'm just not prioritizing them. It's hard to keep all these habits up to snuff.

Chana: But not hard for Billy?

Jason: Oh. I bet it's so much harder for Billy. He's obese and tired and depressed. I guess his excuses are better than mine. But…

Chana: But what?

Jason: But that's why he needs to change.

Chana: Turn it around.

Jason: That's why I need to change?

Chana: How's that true?

Jason: Because if I get too fat and tired I might end up like Billy. Oh ,wait! He's like a warning signal to me.

Chana: Exactly. A Guide Post. Showing you the way forward.

Jason: So when I make excuses for not taking care of my health I'm paving the way towards a life I don't want.

Chana: So what do you want?

Jason: I want to be healthy. I don't want to be diabetic like Dad or a mess like Billy. And I want to have energy to accomplish all the projects I'm working on. And to be with my kids and hopefully grandkids.

Chana: How can you do that?

Jason: First off, by exercising.

Chana: When do you want to exercise?

Jason: At least three times a week. I like going on hikes in the forest, so that feels like a good way to do it.

Chana: How can you fit that into your schedule?

Jason: I'll block out three mornings a week for that.

Chana: What else do you want to do?

Jason: Eat healthier. I just got a picture in my head of all the McDonald's wrappers I've cleaned up from Billy's floor. It grosses me out to see them there, but I eat fast food a few times a week. I can stop that.

Chana: And do what?

Jason: You're going to laugh.

Chana: What?

Jason: My wife makes these awesome smoothies, but I often skip out on them to have a McMuffin. That's an easy switch if I'm honest with myself. I can have the smoothies instead. That would make a huge difference and it's an easy first step.

Jason and I continued to review each item on his list. He clarified steps he could take to live in integrity with his values. Though he had a challenge ahead of him, he felt emboldened to change the only person he has the power to change: himself. He was relieved to see he didn't have to take responsibility for Billy's choices and life circumstances, but could instead shift the way he treated his brother and himself.

TUNING IN

Now it's your turn to practice using your **Guideposts.** Look at the turnarounds you've written for one of your beliefs. Ask yourself: What values are embedded in this turnaround? How can I live in alignment with my values? What tangible steps can I take to bring these ideas into action? If applicable, take out your calendar and schedule your action steps, write the message you've been avoiding, or make the difficult phone call. You know you're living with integrity when your actions match your beliefs. So don't delay!

To learn more about **Guideposts,**
access **Free Bonus Materials** at
ChanaMason.com/Inner-Voices-Bonus.

Acknowledgements

I often walk out of sessions with clients on a high. "Dave!" I'll say to my husband. "I got this new insight!" That's when Dave will say, "Did you write it down?"

"Na… I'll remember it."

"No you won't," he'll say. (It's annoying being married to someone who's always right.)

So, begrudgingly, I'll open my laptop and take a few notes on a new tool I created, a lesson I learned, or a novel way of teaching a concept. All those notes have piled up, and *Inner Voices* is one of the fruits of listening to my husband's sage advice.

Thanks Dave, for being such a rock in my life, for your editorial advice, and for cheering me on.

I'd also like to thank all the beta readers who gave this book the nips and tucks it needed to finally go to print: Susie Zein, Danielle Mumar, Anne Babcox, Chava Levy, Paul Soffe, Rina Hoffman, and M'nucha Bialik.

Thanks to the incredible women of Nachlaot who created a sacred space to learn Inquiry together and support each other through thick and thin.

To my clients (you know who you are) for blossoming so beautifully before my eyes and for bringing me the lessons I need to learn.

To the Holy One, thanks for blessing my life with abundance and light.

Thanks to my son, Aryeh Lev for your endless patience, love, and confidence.

And thank you, dear reader, for inspiring me to write this book in the first place! I'd love to hear your insights and feedback. Be in touch with me at **Chana@ChanaMason.com**.

Did you enjoy Inner Voices?

Keep reading for a preview of

The Size of Your Dreams

Chapter One

The New Math

"*What is my goal in taking this class?*" Jarod Miller stared at the sheet in his hands, eyebrows shooting up. "What kind of math test is this?"

"I never called it a math test," Mr. Griffin said.

Trigonometry had been a disaster ever since Mr. Higgs suffered a stroke in late September. They'd transferred as many students as possible into Mrs. Northrup's class but had to stop when they hit the 30 student limit. During the weeks since, the school shuffled in a stream of substitutes, and most of the remaining students dropped out, leaving just four of us, all seniors. None of us knew where they dug up Mr. Griffin.

Despite there only being four of us left, Jarod moved right past me to the back of the room, because Jarod always sat in the back. His hair still had that just-got-out-of-bed rustle, though it was already fifth period. Stout and muscular, ahe could have been an athlete but gave up sports years ago when he gave up everything else school related. His main workouts now came behind a lawnmower or snow blower.

"Oh no!" Christy Mendez walked in and took a paper. "You're handing out a test? That's so unfair."

"Is there a problem, Christy?"

"You know my name?"

"Yes, I know all of your names." Mr. Griffin's piercing blue eyes caught each of ours. I couldn't help but look away. "Now the problem?"

"You haven't taught us anything yet."

"Agreed. This is to make sure we change that."

Christy mouthed to Jarod, "you've got to be kidding me" and eased into the seat next to his. She eyed Mr. Griffin as she pulled her coffee-colored hair into a ponytail. Besides being captain of the girls' swim team, Christy studied harder than almost anyone. She was sizing up this new guy—she needed trig to get into college.

Darnell Jones lugged himself in, sweaty and winded, just as the bell rang. Jarod liked to joke that Darnell and Billy Jenks were playing a chess match to see who would graduate the fattest, with Billy playing the white pieces, and Darnell, one of only a handful of African Americans in school, playing the black. Darnell squeezed his oversized frame into the desk next to mine and tipped a quick nod in my direction.

"Whatever you call this paper, isn't the answer obvious?" Jarod asked.

"Is it, Jarod? Perhaps I've underestimated you. Today is, after all, my first day teaching. How about you go ahead and fill it out, and we'll see how obvious it is. Fifteen minutes should be enough."

Mr. Griffin sat atop one of the student desks, reading off some note cards and mumbling to himself. He was a surprisingly tall figure. Trimly cropped black hair topped his lean face. He wore a raven-black dress shirt and khakis that fell smoothly over his loafers. His legs pumped back and forth, showing off purple polka-dotted socks.

"Not looking good," Jarod whispered to Christy. "Even I can read without moving my lips."

It only took me a few seconds to answer the question. When I finished, everyone except Darnell had stopped writing. A moment later, his pencil hit the table as well.

Mr. Griffin was so immersed in his notecards, he didn't even notice we were all done. "Uh, Mr. Griffin?" I said.

He looked up from his cards. "Yes, Kelvin? Do you need me to clarify the assignment?"

"No. It's just…. We're all done."

"All of you?" He scanned the room. "Already?"

"Well, yeah," Darnell said. "The question was kind of easy."

"Was it? Personally, I consider it to be quite difficult. But pass back your papers. Let's see how you've all done."

Jarod grabbed Christy's and stretched forward to pass theirs up to me. With three rows of empty chairs between us, I still had to get up to take them. I grabbed Darnell's on my way back and handed all four to Mr. Griffin.

"Darnell," Mr. Griffin said, "you wrote that your goal this year is to learn trigonometry. Why is that important to you?

Darnell shrugged. "It's important stuff to know."

"Is it? Can you give me one example of how you anticipate using trigonometry later in your life?"

Darnell wiped his forehead with the back of his sleeve. "Uh…"

"Your homework, Darnell, will be to ask your parents what math skills they still use and try to ascertain in what grade they learned them. The answer might surprise you."

Mr. Griffin turned to my test. "Kelvin, your goal is to learn how to think better. Are you saying that trigonometry is like a game to test your mind?"

"Yeah, sort of," I said. "It helps you think analytically."

"And do you believe trigonometry is the most effective tool available for teaching analytical thinking? Do you find that math pushes you to your intellectual limits, Kelvin?"

"Not really. I usually get A's without trying too hard."

Jarod scoffed behind me.

"Oh leave him alone, Jarod," Christy said. "It may not come as easy for me as for Kelvin, but I'm also here to get an A."

"Indeed," Mr. Griffin said, "getting an A was what you listed as your goal. Why is that important to you?"

"I need to get a scholarship for college."

"Come on, Christy," Jarod said, "if you get a scholarship it's going to be for your swimming. You're better off working on your breaststroke."

"Grades can play a role too, especially at the better schools. Besides, now that coach is gone, I doubt my times will improve any."

"And you, Jarod?" Mr. Griffin said. "Care to share with the class what you wrote?"

"I'm here for one reason and one reason only. To graduate. I need one more math credit before they'll let me out of this place."

"So your goal in this class is just to get through it?"

"Pretty much."

"Well, it's nice to know that each of you has such low expectations," Mr. Griffin said. "That certainly takes pressure off me. I expect we can achieve most of that quite easily."

Low expectations? Collectively we'd said that we wanted to learn the subject matter, strengthen our thinking abilities, get good grades, and fulfill our educational requirements. What else were we in school for? I raised my hand, but didn't wait to be called on before saying, "What about you, Mr. Griffin? You seem unimpressed with our goals for the class. What are yours?"

"I'm glad you asked, Kelvin." Mr. Griffin picked up a notecard from his desk and read:

> My goal for my trigonometry class is to instill in my students a glimpse of the greatness they have within them and to provide tools to help them succeed in life: emotionally, physically, spiritually, and financially.

"What the…" Jarod mumbled so quietly I couldn't hear the rest of his words. Darnell said, "Isn't one of your goals to teach us math?"

"Oh right, I should probably add that." Mr. Griffin grabbed a pen and wrote below his other goals. He then read out:

> And get all students to master the State approved curriculum for this class.

At this point, we were speechless. Mr. Griffin passed back our papers. "You all filled these out quite quickly the first time. Take the rest of today's class and tonight to rethink your answers. That will be your homework. Darnell, remember you have an additional assignment, to check with your parents regarding the math they use in their lives."

* * *

My 12-year-old sister Megan dragged her feet across the floor as she came in for dinner. Random strings of dirty-blond hair fluttered out of her braid.

"Everything okay at school, sweetie?" Mom placed her hand on Megan's shoulder, but she slunk out of reach.

"It was fine." My sister slid into her chair.

Mom served us chicken, peas, and mashed potatoes. I got a double serving of the mash, my favorite.

She turned to me. "How about you? How was school?"

"Fine. We finally got a new math teacher," I said, before shoving a forkful of chicken into my mouth.

"So perhaps you'll be able to learn trig this year, after all."

"Maybe," I mumbled.

"You don't like him?"

"I dunno. He's kinda weird. I still wish I was in calculus this year."

"This again?" My father asked, glancing up from his research study. It was his fault that I was in trig this year rather than in calculus. When the rest of the advanced math class had gone on to trig last year, he insisted that I take Stats instead. "Statistics are key to understanding data, and data is everywhere. A recent study by the New England Journal of Medicine showed that 5 out of 4 doctors don't understand basic statistics, and they're supposed to be scientists." Dad grinned at his own joke. "You'll thank me for it one day."

I wasn't feeling too thankful at the moment, but I kept my mouth shut. As a neurobiology professor, Dad used statistics all the time in his work, so I couldn't deny their value. But had I taken trig with the rest of my class I could be in calculus now with a normal teacher, rather than stuck with Mr. Griffin.

"How is the new teacher weird?" Mom always broke in with a change of subject when Dad and I got to arguing.

"I dunno, Mom, just weird, okay?"

My mom, as usual, let the subject drop. Megan piped in, "Weird like you, maybe?"

"Shut up, Megan."

I was more curious about this new teacher than I let on to my family. That night I quickly worked through my homework for my other subjects, then dived into math. I didn't spend any time thinking over Mr. Griffin's idiotic question, though. No math teacher showed up the first day of class and forgot he was supposed to be teaching us math. There was something strange about this guy, and I intended to find out what it was.

The problem was, Griffin wasn't such an uncommon name, and teachers weren't known to leave deep digital footprints. Still, one of my counselors at Hacker Camp used to say that with enough skill and perseverance, you could find information on anyone. I'd been programming since before I could ride a bike, so no issue with my computer skills. And my parents almost never checked on me after I went to bed, so as long as I didn't make too much noise, I could stay up all night if I had to.

I had two computers in my room (one a Mac, the other an old PC that I'd converted to Linux) and a total of four monitors. I powered them all on and prepared to dig in. The school website didn't have him listed, but I found a notice on the Superintendent's site mentioning he'd been hired to take over Mr. Higgs' trigonometry class for the rest of the year. That was odd; I assumed he'd take over all of Mr. Higgs' classes, but it was just ours. More importantly, I got the piece of information I'd been looking for: his first name. It is far easier to search for people with unusual names—you don't get so many false positives. So when I saw that his first name was Mark, I knew I was out of luck.

I pulled up a digital notepad and typed in all I knew. It wasn't much. His name was far too common to be of much use. He was only part-time at the school and had just started teaching there, so he likely hadn't even updated his LinkedIn profile with the school name yet—if he even had one. He was teaching math, but this bizarre first day made me doubt he'd ever taught before, much less have a teaching degree. The one thing I felt confident about was location. He wouldn't commute more than 30 miles to get to some part-time teaching job. There were no more than ten towns within that radius, so I'd start by searching his name followed by each of the town names until I found all of the Mark Griffins living in this part of the state.

I dragged my notepad to my secondary monitor and opened a browser on my main one. Though I knew it was pointless, I started off with just the most general search, typing only his name into the search bar.

And there he was. Just like that. First page, first result. I knew it was the same Mark Griffin because Google posted a picture of him in the right column, along with a link to his Wikipedia page. His Wikipedia page? He must be the first teacher in the history of our school, perhaps the first teacher of *any* school, with his own Wikipedia page.

Ding. It was Darnell on chat.

"Hey," he wrote. "Some first day of math, eh?"

"No kidding. How are you doing?"

"Still reeling from last night's game. I can't believe I didn't start Gurley."

I didn't share Darnell's love of football, but I nonetheless let him talk me into joining his fantasy league. I hadn't even checked the scores yet this week. "He had a good game?"

"198 yards and two touchdowns. Man, I wish I could run like that."

As the fattest, slowest kid I knew, Darnell could barely run down the hall, much less a football field. I ignored his comment, and typed, "BTW, Mr. Griffin has his own Wikipedia page."

"No way!!!!" Darnell wrote. "Send me the link."

I copied and pasted it over, then dived into the article. Turns out he studied machine learning and artificial intelligence at MIT, the same school I was hoping to attend. Then he went to work building high-volume stock market trading machines for some investment bank I'd never heard of. He left after three years and began a data mining startup, apparently self-funding it with earnings from his banking job. Last year he sold the company to Oracle.

"It says he sold his business for some undisclosed amount," Darnell wrote. "How much do you think that is?"

"No clue, but enough that he doesn't need the salary from a part-time teaching job."

"So what's he doing here?"

"Your guess is as good as mine." I sent the link to Christy and Jarod, who despite not having much to do with me in school were still my Facebook "friends." I pulled out the "test" from math class where I'd written that my goal was "To learn how to think better." It was such an obvious answer at the time, though Mr. Griffin had been unimpressed.

As much as he seemed like a kook in class, everything I'd just learned about Mr. Griffin made me wonder, what should my answer be?

Chapter Two

The Power of Incentives

"You're staring." Wally elbowed my arm.

I'd just finished my sandwich, and my eyes had wandered over to Christy's table. Where Monica Gray sat. My attention quickly found its way back to the apple in my hand. "No, I'm not."

"Kelvin, who do you think you're kidding? She doesn't even know your name."

"Sure she does. We had lab together last year."

"You had lab with who?"

"Monica."

"You mean the girl you *weren't* staring at?" Wally slapped his leg and chortled. He was the only kid in school who could program as well as I could, and he always looked for opportunities to outsmart me.

"Ha ha," I said, wanting to bring the conversation to an end as quickly as I could. I also enjoyed one-upping Wally, and of the two of us, I had the sharper wit. But Monica was turning in our direction now. It was bad enough that my face was breaking out worse than ever today. Being seen hanging out with Wally Hoster, whose hair was so greasy he could shape it without gel, was enough to earn social exile. Mind, I was already sitting next to him, but that was just because it beat sitting alone. Barely.

"There's no point anyway." Bits of egg salad sprayed out of Wally's mouth as he spoke. "It's not like she's gonna follow you to MIT."

* * *

When Jarod sat down in the second to last row, I knew my message about Mr. Griffin had piqued his interest. Christy sat in the desk in front of him. Even Darnell made a special effort to get to class before the bell, which left him sweatier than usual.

Mr. Griffin sat at his desk reading his notecards. When the bell rang, he put them down and stepped to the front of the class.

"Darnell, tell us about your homework."

Darnell was still huffing when he said, "I asked my folks what math they used, and the only things they could think of were addition, subtraction, multiplication, division, and fractions, all of which they learned by the 5th grade."

"Interesting. What do—?"

"Wait," he put up his hand, "there's more. Then I called my uncle. He couldn't think of any time he used advanced math either, but my aunt said she uses it in her job every day."

"And what does she do?"

Darnell grinned. "She's a high school math teacher."

Mr. Griffin raised an eyebrow. "So what do you take away from all of this?"

Darnell huffed out one final breath. "I'm mostly confused. Usually, teachers try to get us more interested in their subjects, you seem to want us to be less interested."

"Not at all. I just want you to understand the limitations of the curriculum alone."

I broke in. "The school must consider the curriculum valuable. Otherwise, they wouldn't require it."

Jarod scoffed. "The curriculum is like a hundred years old. It's not like they update it for the times."

"Don't discard something just because it's old," Mr. Griffin said. "The techniques I use every day are more than a hundred years old, and I've still never found anything more potent. Nonetheless, I agree that mastering the material in your classes is no longer the ticket to success or even employment that it once was."

"Does this mean you're not going to teach us math?" Christy asked.

"I've been hired to be your math teacher. Despite what others may think of my techniques, I always live up to my obligations. Speaking of which, I'd like hear how all of you expanded on yesterday's assignment."

I bit my lip. Despite my late-night efforts, I hadn't added a word to my page. Judging from the silence in the room, I wasn't alone.

After a painfully long delay, Mr. Griffin said, "I see." He slowly paced down one of the empty aisles of the classroom, rolling a pen between his fingers.

When he reached the last desk, he punctured the air with the pen. "I've got it. I know why you're all struggling to put effort into yesterday's assignment."

"Because it's ridiculously easy?" Jarod suggested.

"No, because it's ridiculously hard. It was unfair of me to give you such a task on day one. Indeed, I see now that I violated one of my core principles."

"Which is what?" Christy asked.

"To always start with vision. I tried, but I defined my question far too narrowly to get you there."

Jarod stretched his hands out before him and moved them around an imaginary orb. Speaking with the thick accent of a fortune teller at a fair, he said, "I envision passing trigonometry so I can get out of this school."

"Precisely," Mr. Griffin said. "All you want to do is leave school because you have no compelling vision of what you want to get from school."

Jarod's hands dropped. He stared back, silent.

"Does that mean," Darnell said, "that you want to change the question from what we hope to get out of trigonometry to what we hope to get out of school?"

"No, no, no Darnell, it's still too narrow. How can you know what you want to get out of school without first knowing what you want out of life?"

Mr. Griffin was practically bouncing, but I couldn't share his enthusiasm.

"I totally know what I want to do," Christy said. "I want to become a physical therapist."

"Very good. If you know what you want to do for a living, you're already ahead of most. But I don't just want a vision for your job—I want a vision for your *life*. That includes a vision for your home, family, and community. For how you spend time *outside* of work, not just *in* it."

"Ugh." Christy rolled her eyes and crossed her arms. "Why is it that whenever a woman brings up career, the automatic response is that she has to think about family?"

"As a woman, it's more likely that you've at least given it some thought," Mr. Griffin said. "Most men never give family a moment's consideration until it's too late."

"How's it ever too late?" Darnell asked.

Mr. Griffin sighed. "I can't tell you how many of my peers spent a fortune in tuition and years of their lives pursuing careers that only lasted two or three years because they suddenly had a family and found their jobs incompatible."

Christy's arms unclenched.

I thought about my own plans. I always dreamed of working for some hard-core start-up. The programmers I met who'd gone down that path didn't just work 80 hour weeks, they bragged about it. Somehow, I'd never given any thought to having a family at the same time. Did I really want to have kids but never see them?

"So how am I supposed to get a vision for my life?" Darnell asked.

"Here's a very simple exercise. Close your eyes. Go on Jarod—I'm not going to throw anything at you. Good. Take three slow, deep breaths."

My body sank deeper into my seat.

Mr. Griffin's voice grew softer. "Now, imagine yourself twenty years in the future. You're happy. Life has been good to you. You feel tremendously grateful that everything has fallen into place. Look around you."

"All I see is an empty math class," Jarod said.

"Eyes closed, Jarod. I want you to visualize your future. What does your life look like?" He paused. I immediately saw an image of working at a startup. "Are you married?"

My initial thought was yes, but I couldn't envision that.

"Do you have children? Where do you live? What do you do? How do you contribute to others?" The questions came faster now, and while visions flashed across my mind, I couldn't hold all of them. "Open your eyes, and write down what you saw."

Mr. Griffin paced back to his chair, sat down, and propped his heels up on his desk. He pulled a tattered book out of his briefcase. I tilted my head to get a look at the cover. *Think and Grow Rich.* He opened to a dog-eared page in the middle of the tome and said, "You have until the end of class."

The first thing I wrote about was my career. That part was easy. I knew I wanted to create world-changing technologies. Like Tesla. Not Tesla now, with its billions of dollars in income, but like Tesla when they first started out.

As to where I'd live, that was also easy. There were really only a few options for that type of work. Silicon Valley, Seattle, Austin. I'd put down Austin for now; it was more up and coming.

That's when I got stuck. *Marriage? Children? Community?*

I put down my pen and looked around the class. Mr. Griffin was still absorbed in his book. Christy was bent over her paper, had already written a full page, and was still going strong. Jarod was leaning back, playing with his Leatherman. His sheet of paper was glaringly white for its blankness. Darnell had his pen close to the top of his page and was staring up at the ceiling, looking for answers.

I returned to my own paper. *Why was this so difficult?* Not a day went by when I didn't think about having more friends, and hardly an hour when I didn't think about having a girlfriend. That's really all Mr. Griffin had asked us to do, to think about what we wanted in life. So why was I all of a sudden drawing a blank?

* * *

The next morning, I dragged myself out of bed and moved through the house like a soggy mop. My mother eyed me all through breakfast, but she knew better than to ask me questions that early in the day. Megan read her Kindle while she ate, paying me no mind.

I had flitted in and out of sleep the night before, haunted by a recurring dream about living at some high-tech start-up with a blow-up mattress, a nightlight, and a teddy bear stored under my cubicle desk. I spent dark, cold nights there alone with only microwave pizza to keep me company. Everything felt so incredibly normal, but I woke up in sweats each time the microwave beeped that the pizza was ready. Was this my future?

I had a hard time keeping my eyes, or even my mind, open during the first few hours of the day. By the time fifth period came around, I was ready to crawl into the janitor's closet and use *his* mop as a pillow. Beside my exhaustion was the uneasy feeling that I'd have to revisit my nightmare during Mr. Griffin's class. Plus, I hadn't completed his assignment. I never did that.

"Okay, what have you all got?" Mr. Griffin said as soon as we were all seated. "Jarod?"

"This assignment was lame." The thick rubber soles of his work-boots drummed against the leg of his desk. "What kinda math class is this anyhow?"

"Lame," Mr. Griffin said. "I see…So, you don't have any plans for your future?"

"Just the same crap as everyone else. College, job, wife, kids, house, retire, die. What's there to write?"

Mr. Griffin looked at the rest of us. "You all have something like this?"

"More or less…," Christy's shoulders rose to meet her ears. She'd written a hundred times more than Jarod and ten times more than I had. Did everything she jotted down really get summed up by Jarod in just a few words? Mine didn't even get that far.

"I thought our visions were pretty lame," Jarod said, "but you seem mighty impressed."

Mr. Griffin indeed was practically bouncing at the front of the class. "Impressed? Hardly. I'm excited by their very lameness."

"You like lame?" Christy asked.

"Absolutely. It tells me that, like most people, you've never given much thought to your life goals."

"And that's good?" I asked.

"For me it is. I don't teach for the benefits, and certainly not for the salary.

I'm here because I want to create lasting change. Frankly, I'm new at this. I had no idea how easy or hard this would be. But now that I see you've all set the bar so low, I do not doubt that I can completely revolutionize your lives this year."

Mr. Griffin may have been grinning from ear to ear, but we couldn't share his enthusiasm. Was he really telling us all that we were pathetic and mindless? And this was *good* news because he was going to somehow fix us?

"You still didn't answer my question." Jarod kicked the legs of his desk. "What does this have to do with math?"

"If I do my job well, you'll find within yourself the ability to go as far as you want with your mathematics. Nonetheless, my core goal as your teacher is not confined to math."

Christy leaned forward in her chair. "So what is your goal?"

"My goal is to activate your minds, to give you the tools to succeed no matter what direction you take."

If I hadn't read the article on him the other night, I wouldn't have given his words much credence. But this guy was no stranger to success.

Jarod, however, was more interested in what it would cost him. "You're going to do this by the end of the year, *on top* of teaching us math? Just how much homework do you plan on giving us?"

"Five minutes a day."

"Five minutes? That's it?"

"That's all it will take to implement my basic techniques. Beyond that, I expect you'll each want to push yourselves to do more. But those will be *your* steps toward *your* goals, not mine."

"What are these techniques?" I asked. "You said they were a hundred years old?"

"If you dig deep enough, you'll find variations in use even thousands of years ago. But the first time I know they were written down was in 1937."

"Who wrote them?"

"Napoleon Hill."

Jarod scoffed. "That French dude?"

Christy slapped his shoulder. "That was Napoleon Bonaparte. We just learned about him in European history last year. Where were you?"

"Who's Napoleon Hill?" I asked.

Mr. Griffin sat on his desk. "Ever heard of Andrew Carnegie?"

"As in Carnegie Hall?" Christy asked.

"Wasn't he a Robber Baron?" I asked.

"You're both right. He started out as a penniless immigrant, working twelve hour days for $1.20 a week. He worked his way up to become one of the wealthiest men in the world, then spent the latter portion of his life giving most of it away. He built Carnegie Hall as well as countless libraries around the world."

"What does he have to do with this Napoleon guy?" Darnell asked.

"Carnegie gave the young Napoleon Hill a task, and Hill spent the next 25 years completing it."

"What was the task?" I asked.

"To study the elements of success."

"So he studied successful people?" I asked.

"Not only. It wasn't enough to find commonalities among the successful. He also had to find what distinguished them from those he deemed failures."

"Those notecards you read," Jarod nodded to the cards next to Mr. Griffin. "They come from him?"

"They're my own practice, but I developed them by applying the principles I learned from Napoleon Hill."

"Let me guess," Jarod kicked his desk extra hard. "You want to fix our goals, and then I suppose you'll have us write them down on notecards?"

Mr. Griffin grinned like the Cheshire cat. "No, I want *you* to fix your goals." He leaned in toward Jarod. "We'll go over the steps of creating truly compelling goals for your life, as well as how to reinforce them so that they stick. That's where the notecards come in."

"How do they work?" Darnell asked. Was he actually excited by this?

"There are three components of the Outcome Cards. The first is your goal, the second is your deadline, and the third is the list of steps you'll take to hit that goal."

"Can you give us an example?" Darnell asked again.

"Certainly." Mr. Griffin picked up his stack of notecards, pulled one out and read:

> I intend to bring my marathon time down to three hours and fifteen minutes or below by April 16, in time for the Boston Marathon. To do this, I will 1) run at least four days per week, 2) run at least a half-marathon distance every Sunday, 3) weight train on my non-running days, 4) reward myself each time I break my fastest time, and 5) book additional training sessions with my coach whenever my average time drops.

"You run marathons?" Christy asked.

"I'm starting to. I want to compete in Ironman as well, but one thing at a time."

"So you're just supposed to let this piece of paper dictate what you do?" Jarod asked.

Mr. Griffin walked straight to Jarod's desk and slapped his notecard down on it. "Who wrote the note, Jarod?"

"I guess you did."

"And who developed the steps on the card?"

"Looks like the same handwriting to me…"

"Good to see you're paying attention," Mr. Griffin said. "So, who is dictating to whom?"

"I get your point, but still…." Jarod flicked his hand in the air. "It's like school—just having to follow more directions. Why should you have a notecard at all? Can't you just do what you want without it?"

"Yes, but I'm hardly consistent. Some days I want one thing, other days it's something else. That's why most people make such little progress in their lives. They never build momentum."

"This is ludicrous," Christy said. "Say one day I think I want to study law, and the next day I change my mind to medicine. You're saying that because I wrote law down on the notecard that I should stick with it?"

"Truthfully Christy, how often do you waffle between two burning desires?"

Christy shifted in her chair. "It happens sometimes."

"If you have even one burning desire, you're well ahead of the pack. Most people simply focus on getting through the day, the week, the semester, or whatever it is. To use your example, you'd be more likely to waffle between a vague idea that you'd sort of like to study law and another vague idea that you kinda think medicine would be better."

Jarod picked up Mr. Griffin's card and flapped it back and forth before him. "And these notecards are supposed to change that?"

"Absolutely. The present moment is like twilight. The past behind you is bright and clear, but the future ahead is a masked in darkness. Making an Outcome Card is like shining a beam of light into that darkness."

"You're telling me this card is going to predict my future?" Jarod asked.

"Your future is not set—there are infinite possibilities before you. The card helps you hone in on the future you choose to pursue."

"What if we make the card at the wrong time?" Darnell asked.

"What do you mean, the wrong time?"

"Well, like Christy said, sometimes you want law, other times medicine. What if you make the notecard during a time when you're thinking law, but you're better suited to medicine?"

"Excellent question, Darnell. That's why we make the cards during times of clarity."

"Like when?" Christy asked.

"Clarity most often comes at the extremes: when you're on top of the world and want to stay there, or when you hit rock bottom and want to pick yourself up. The problem is that these moments are fleeting."

"So we make the cards to remind us of the goals we made during those times of clarity?" I asked.

"Exactly. Then they keep us on track during the blah moments. For me, sometimes I want to train for the marathon; other times I'd rather sit on the couch with a beer and watch football. The notecards may be my voice, but they're my voice of vision. Any time that I think of skipping my workout, I read my card, and it's like my higher-self whispering in my ear."

"But isn't it possible," I asked, "that you can have a moment of clarity and still be wrong? Can't you have a rock bottom moment, say when you're struggling in biology, and suddenly see that it would be so much better to study law. What happens if you make my notecard and law isn't for you after all? Maybe you're best off sticking it through with medicine, or switching to engineering?"

"The notecards help you clarify that as well. Just because you write them doesn't mean that you're stuck with them for life. When I read my cards, I normally hear the voice of my higher-self. I know the goals on my card are what I want, and reading them helps me to refocus my energy. But periodically, when I read a card the goal doesn't move me at all. I don't hear the voice of my higher-self, I hear only delusion."

"What do you do then?" Christy asked.

"I tear up the card."

Christy's brow creased. She'd never given up on anything. "Just like that?"

"Normally I'll wait a day or two to make sure the feeling is consistent. Otherwise, I'd be in danger of trashing all my goals every time I get into a bad mood. But if nothing shifts, I tear it up."

Darnell picked at his cuticles, something he usually did during tests. "So if you keep not liking what the card says, you know you've set the wrong goal?"

"Or the wrong steps or the wrong date. Once you learn how to interpret your emotional reactions, they'll guide you toward your true goals as well as the ideal path to manifest them."

* * *

The next day, we rehashed our questions from the day before, even though we knew the answers. I wasn't the only one still trying to get my head around the concept. One thing that had become clear, Mr. Griffin said, "is that you guys aren't ready to work on a greater vision for your lives. At this point, it's best to choose one small goal to focus on."

Late in the class, Jarod raised his hand. "Mr. Griffin, perhaps if there were some grade incentives tied to the cards it would help us try them out."

"Grade incentives?" Mr. Griffin asked.

Darnell perked up. "Yeah, like if we got an automatic A in math if we made these cards and stuck to them."

Mr. Griffin raised his eyebrows. "For the opportunity to help you get your life on track, I have to give you an automatic A?"

Jarod said, "It doesn't have to be an A. but an incentive would certainly help us stick to it."

The bell rang. "I'll think your idea over, Jarod. See you all tomorrow."

"Remind me, what were we talking about yesterday?" Mr. Griffin asked with a grin as we took our seats the next day.

"Grade incentives," Jarod said. "You said you'd think them over."

"And I did. Do you really feel that an incentive would help you make and stick to the cards?"

"Yes," Jarod said.

"Does everyone feel this way?"

The rest of us said, "Yes."

"It's not enough to just read them in math class. The most important times to read your cards are first thing in the morning to set your intentions for the day, and immediately before bed, so they truly penetrate your unconscious mind. To see their effectiveness, you'll have to commit to doing this for at least 30 days. Are you all willing to do that?"

We all said, "Yes."

"The problem is, how will I know if you've done them? If there's a grade incentive, then there's also an incentive to lie."

"We can use an app," I suggested. "Each time we read our card, we check off the app. You'll get a notice with the time we did it."

"Interesting idea, Kelvin, but what if one of you claims you read the card but forgot to check off the app?"

Christy said, "We can put a note on the bottom of our cards saying 'check off the app.' Then if there's no check on the app, you'll know we didn't do it."

"Does everyone agree that if the app does not report that you read off the card, you won't get credit for reading it that time?" Mr. Griffin asked.

We agreed.

"Very well. I found an app that would work last night. I'll send you the link after class."

"Wait," I said. "You already thought about an app?"

"Once you brought up grade incentives, it made sense to have a way to keep track."

"Then why didn't you tell us about it?"

"I'm not here to give you answers, but to help you work them out. Didn't it feel better to come up with the solution on your own?"

I was annoyed at his ploy but had to admit that it had felt good when I made the suggestion. "I suppose great minds think alike."

"In my experience, it's the opposite," Mr. Griffin said. "Extraordinary minds are original. Ordinary minds think alike. Or perhaps I should say that those who don't actively grow their minds think alike, for every human mind can be extraordinary."

Was he calling me ordinary? Or insinuating that I wasn't growing my mind?

"Does this mean you'll do the grade incentives?" Jarod asked.

"I'm willing to give them a shot. But on two conditions. One, I'm only going to offer them to those students who genuinely feel the grade incentives will help them. Intrinsic motivation always trumps incentives in my mind. But I will give it as a tool for those who need it. How many of you feel you need this?"

At this point, I was already curious to try out the cards. While I understood his point about intrinsic motivation, I wasn't dumb enough to turn down a grade incentive. I eagerly raised my hand with the rest of the class.

"Fine. It can apply to all of you. Second, I will only do it for students who will commit, right now, that once you have a card, you will read it twice a day for 30 days. Even though you don't have your cards yet, once you commit, there is no backing out. Whoever doesn't wish to commit can still participate at their own pace, but will not qualify for the grade incentives. Who is ready to commit right now?"

Again, all of us raised our hands.

"Very well, then I have a contract for you all to sign. Get in line and sign one by one."

Mr. Griffin brought out a bunch of papers from his desk. "I've already signed my name and dated these. You just need to sign and print your names below."

The pages he held were full of text, written in what looked like 8 point font.

Darnell got up to the desk first and signed his name in the tiny space between the end of the text and the bottom of the page. I was next. The text began, "This is a contract between Mr. Griffin (herein "Mr. Griffin" or "teacher") and the students in his fifth-period trigonometry class (herein "student" or "students")…"

It would take me a full ten minutes to read the entire thing; maybe more, as it seemed all written in legalese. Sensing Jarod's impatience behind me, I quickly signed my name at the bottom as Darnell had. Neither Jarod nor Christy wasted their time with even trying to read over the text, just signed and returned to their seats.

Darnell seemed particularly pleased. "This is going to be the easiest math class ever! I can't believe I get an A for just reading this notecard twice a day."

"An A?" Mr. Griffin placed the signed contracts in a drawer, locked it, and dropped the key in his pocket. "That wasn't the agreement."

"Sure it was," Darnell said. "We talked about it yesterday."

"You suggested that yesterday. But the grade incentives weren't your idea—they were Jarod's. He was clear that the incentive didn't have to be an automatic A."

"So I'll still have to study math?" Darnell asked. "Bummer. But at least it should help. What do I get, another ten points on my average or something?"

"You don't get anything, Darnell. You lose points if you don't follow through."

"Lose points?" Jarod said. "That wasn't our deal."

"Of course it was. It was written very clearly on the contract you all signed."

"But we didn't even read the contracts."

"I noticed. Would you like to read them now?" Mr. Griffin handed around unsigned contracts, keeping the signed ones safely locked in his desk.

"Wait." Christy's eyes bulged over her copy. "I lose five points on my overall grade every time I forget to read my card?"

"Even if you remember to read the card, but forget to check the app," Mr. Griffin said. "Remember, that was your suggestion."

Heat rose to my cheeks. "If we forget more than five times we fail math?"

"Correct. Remember, I only gave this option to those who asked for a grade incentive. I always prefer intrinsic motivation. But you thought this would help you, so I offered it as a tool."

"A tool?" I said. "It sounds more like a punishment."

"Punishments, or the threat of them, can be great tools. You're all old enough to drive. How many of you try to stay within the speed limit?"

Silence.

"How many of you regularly go more than 20 miles per hour over the speed limit?"

Jarod raised his hand.

"The rest of you, what keeps you from driving that fast?"

"Over 20 miles an hour the tickets are like $160," Christy said.

"Yeah," Darnell said, "and my dad would take away my driving privileges if he ever caught me going that fast."

"None of you reduce your speed out of concern for safety?" Mr. Griffin asked. No one responded.

"Teenagers." Mr. Griffin shook his head. "Do you see why society holds the threat of punishment over your heads? That's how they keep the roads safe."

A teacher intentionally tricking us into signing an agreement not in our interests? Who does this guy think he is? "I don't think it was fair putting it on the contract and not telling us," I said.

"Kelvin, do you remember what I told you my goals were for this year?"

I clenched my jaw and mumbled, "Something about helping us lead extraordinary lives."

"Precisely. Fairness was not among my goals."

We all groaned.

"Let this be a lesson to you. You must think hard about what you put on your cards because they'll give you laser focus toward these goals. Elements left off of your cards can get squeezed out." Mr. Griffin sat back on his desk. "Like fairness in my case."

"So now we're stuck?" Darnell asked.

"No, you're not stuck."

Darnell sat straighter. "You mean you'll let us take the contracts back?"

"No. That's another lesson I wanted to teach in a way that you'd never forget. You'll each sign hundreds, if not thousands of contracts in your life. Those who give them to you will primarily be looking out for their interests, not yours. Always be aware of what you bind yourself to."

Darnell's eyebrows pinched. "But you said we're not stuck?"

"You're not. You're welcome to transfer to another math class or drop math altogether. It all goes back to your vision for your life, and who you think can best help you get there. Care to transfer, Darnell?"

Darnell exhaled loudly. "No, I'll stay here."

"Anyone else?"

So far, I really couldn't say that I *liked* Mr. Griffin—he was like a mosquito that kept buzzing in my ear. Yet, he was intriguing. I doubted he'd ever bring us to the profound life transformations he promised, but no other teacher had ever attempted to. And…what if he did? Images of my nightmare in the cubicle wafted through my mind. My future vision could use some refining. It was worth a shot.

When no one said they wanted to transfer, Mr. Griffin said, "Just remember that you're not trapped. You're choosing to stay here."

"I still feel stuck to this contract," Darnell said.

"Yes, I know. It's written in your posture. The more ownership you take over your decisions, the straighter you'll sit in your chair. Besides, being stuck is not the worst thing. Sometimes I intentionally get myself stuck."

"Why would you do that?" I asked.

"I do it for motivation, and to force myself to find new answers."

"How can getting stuck motivate you?" Christy asked.

"It's like when Cortez burnt his ships upon landing in Mexico in 1519. The message to his men was clear. You can't back out. Succeed or die. I've used that technique on myself, though with less dire consequences."

"Like when?" Christy asked.

"I used it in college when trying to lose weight."

Darnell's head tilted up. "You, lose weight?" He scanned our lean, muscular teacher with cold eyes.

"You might not guess it looking at me now," Mr. Griffin patted his stomach, "but I used to be over 100 pounds overweight."

"Really?" Darnell was easily that overweight himself. "How did you lose it?"

"I tried diet after diet. I must have lost the same five pounds ten times, but I always put them right back on."

"So how'd you keep them off?"

"I backed myself into a corner. I made sure that I had two options, weight loss or a fate far worse than hunger."

"Like what?" Darnell asked.

"I made a list of all the foods I knew I needed to avoid, and I gave a copy of the list to all of my friends, plus a few people who were anything but my friends. I told them all that if they caught me eating anything on that list, they could make me eat whatever they wanted."

"Anything?"

"Anything that wouldn't injure or kill me. One day I was walking with my friend Andres, and we passed some fresh dog poop on the ground next to a hamburger stand. Andres asked them for a paper plate and a spoon, and scooped the poop onto the plate." Mr. Griffin cringed. "He waved it in front of me, telling me how much fun he was going to have watching me eat it all."

"Gross!" Jarod pretended to puke behind his desk.

"You never did, did you?" Christy asked.

"No. I lost the pounds, and Andres wound up with stale dog poop in his fridge. A couple of times I came close to cheating, and each time all I had to do was think of that plate of dog poop. Just knowing it was there, waiting for me, was enough to keep me on my diet."

The bell rang.

"I trust you've all had a memorable day. Next week we'll start working on your cards. And don't worry. The 30 days haven't even started yet."

"When do they start?" Christy asked.

"Everything will be just like it says on your contract."

"Where?"

Mr. Griffin's smirk returned. "On the other part you didn't read."

Chapter Three

Sink or Swim

I was curled up on the couch reading *The Martian* and trying to avoid thinking about Mr. Griffin and his sleazy contract when Dad walked in. He wore the same old khaki pants and a wrinkled button-down shirt. At least he didn't have acne anymore, though the pockmarks on his face showed that his skin had looked just like mine back in the day.

"Hi Kelvin," he said.

I didn't even look up. "Hey."

"How was school?"

"Fine."

"Liking the new math teacher any more?"

I didn't want to go there. "Eh."

"So…a physicist from London is lecturing at the university about black holes next Friday evening. Want to go?"

While half the senior class was at some party? "Nah."

"You'll be sure to get sucked in."

It took all my strength not to roll my eyes.

"I don't need to know until late in the week. You think about it until then, okay Kelvin?"

"Sure, Dad."

I felt him standing by the doorway, stalling. I guess Dad couldn't think of anything else to say, because after a minute, he continued on towards the kitchen.

* * *

"How about you, Christy. You have something you'd like to work on?"

It was Monday afternoon. Mr. Griffin just got through explaining the "rules." Each of us would start our 30 day period as soon as we chose our goal. He didn't want us to wait too long, or else we'd lose out on precious time. One goal immediately came to my mind, but there was no way I was going to discuss it in front of the class. When asked, I just lied and said I couldn't think of anything. Fortunately, Mr. Griffin moved on to Christy to find his first sucker.

"No, I don't have anything," Christy said.

"Nothing?"

"Nah. I had one, but I gave up on it."

"What was that?" Mr. Griffin asked.

"Last year, when coach appointed me captain of the girls' swim team, I made it my goal to win the State Championship this year."

"Why'd you give up on it?"

"You didn't hear what happened?"

Mr. Griffin rubbed his chin. "Was that the drunk driver?"

Christy nodded and tears collected in her eyes. "Coach was killed the week before school began."

"They haven't given you anyone else?"

"No." Christy shoved her hands into the narrow gap between her crossed legs. "I approached the athletic director, and he said he didn't have the time to get someone new. I learned later that they used most of the budget to get an extra assistant coach for the football team."

"Don't they legally have to give you a coach?"

"Yeah. There's this lady who works as a pool attendant who said she'd be willing to accompany us to meets, so he gave her a tiny salary and appointed her as our official coach. She doesn't do anything though."

"So who runs practice?"

"Jill and I. Jill is my co-captain. But we don't know what we're doing. The older girls aren't making any progress, and the younger ones are completely lost."

Mr. Griffin leaned on the edge of his desk. "Tell me about your coach."

"Coach Silver was amazing. When she made me captain and told me she wanted to win States this year, I actually thought we had a chance."

"And now?"

Christy shook her head. "Now we're hopeless."

Mr. Griffin swept his eyes over the entire class. "You get what you settle for."

Christy's eyes narrowed. "What does that mean?"

"You probably think that you gave up on your goal because it went out of reach. I expect it's the opposite: your goal left your reach because you gave up on it."

"Our coach died!" Christy's tears spilled down her cheeks. Why was Mr. Griffin being so heartless?

"Did you only want to win for the coach?" he asked.

Christy mumbled, "Of course not. For all of us."

"Then why give up just because you lost your coach?"

"We're not giving up. We're just hopeless." A new rush of anguish overcame her.

"*Hopeless*. An interesting choice of language. You didn't say you're incapable. After all, you have the same athletes on the team that you had before your coach died, so if you had the physical capabilities to win before, you've still got them now. As you point out, what's changed is your belief in yourselves. You no longer have hope."

"What's changed," Christy sat up straight and drove her words like daggers, "is that our coach is dead! We're lost without her."

Mr. Griffin kept his cool. "I'm not saying that your path is without challenges. But after all, there's little thrill in achieving easy victories. My goal is to stretch you, to show you that you're capable of achieving so much more than you realize."

"I know what the team is capable of, Mr. Griffin, and the championship is beyond us."

Mr. Griffin sighed and went to the whiteboard. "I want you all to remember this quote." He wrote down:

The Size of your Dreams must always exceed
your current capacity to achieve them.

—*Ellen Johnson Sirleaf*

"Who is she?" Christy asked.

"The first woman ever elected President of an African nation. She also said, 'If your dreams do not scare you, they are not big enough.' She would know about scary dreams. Her efforts to end Liberia's cycle of violence and promote women's rights earned her a Nobel Peace Prize."

"Not all of us are looking to change the world, Mr. Griffin," Christy said.

"Big changes evolve from small changes, Christy. Today, we might only be working on a high school swim team, but you never know what challenge tomorrow brings. Master these tools now, and you'll be prepared to face whatever lies ahead."

Christy sank into her chair and crossed her arms.

Mr. Griffin put down the whiteboard marker. "I know you're all deeply skeptical of my approach. Tell me, Christy, if following my steps leads you to win the State Championship, will I win you over to my methods?"

Christy's head bent to the side. "You serious?"

"You bet. If you won the Championship, would you trust me then?"

"Absolutely."

"I believe it's possible, but only if you're willing to try."

Christy shrugged her shoulders. "I'll try. Why not? You'll fail me anyhow if I don't."

"No, not like that. I'm not talking about putting a toe in the water. I'm talking about going all in, giving me everything you've got."

"I thought you said this was going to only be five minutes a day for 30 days?"

"That's right, your homework from me will only be five minutes a day for 30 days, but I need your complete dedication during those five minutes. Plus, you'll give yourself additional tasks to complete *your* goal. You'll need to put the same dedication into those. Agreed?"

"Okay, I guess."

"This is not a guessing game, Christy. Remember, you get what you settle for. Winning is going to take more dedication than that."

She wiped her eyes with the back of her hands. "I'm dedicated."

Mr. Griffin shook his head. "I don't know. I'm not seeing a girl who's passionate about winning the State Championship."

"What?" Christy slapped her hand against her desk. "How can you say that?"

"You think you have the passion it takes?"

"Absolutely."

"Then if you have the passion and the dedication, come up here."

Christy stepped up to the front of the room.

"Face the class and close your eyes. Go on, no one's going to laugh at you. Good. Now ask yourself, what would it mean to you to lead your team to victory in the State Championship?"

"It would be great."

"Just great? I want you to imagine that you've made it to the Championship and it's neck and neck. What's the last event?"

"The 4 x 100 relay."

"What place are you swimming?"

"Last, I'm the anchor."

"Excellent. So you're standing on the edge of the pool, waiting your turn. The girls on your team are good, but the competition is better. To your left and right, the anchors from the other teams jump into the pool. Finally, your teammate hits the edge of the pool, and you jump in. You're behind, but determined. By the time you finish your first lap, you've caught up to all but two of the swimmers. 50 yards to go. You're halfway through the second lap when you pass the next girl. 25 yards. You're tired. Your arms are burning. But nothing's going to stop you. You draw strength from deep down. 15 yards. She's still ahead. 10 yards. You're getting close. 5 yards. You've pulled even. You reach out and, by a finger's breath, hit the edge of the pool first.

"Can you see it, Christy?"

Christy nodded.

"Can you feel it, Christy?"

"Yes."

"What happens next?"

"The entire team goes crazy. They all jump into the pool and hug me. We're all screaming, some even crying." Christy's eyes swelled.

Mr. Griffin said, "You barely have time to towel off before someone hands you the largest trophy you've ever seen and a microphone. What do you say?"

"I'd take the trophy over to the stands."

"Why? Who's in the stands?"

"Coach Silver's nine-year-old daughter Kim is there, watching with her dad. I'd say, 'we want you to have this, Kim, from all the girls on the team. Whenever you look at it, we want you to remember everything your mom did for us. Without her, we never could have won. And remember all that she did for you. You didn't have her long enough. But with the gifts she gave you, you can do anything!'"

"I want everyone to remember this look on Christy's face. That's the look of inspiration. With the expression she had ten minutes ago, she was barely capable of achieving the ordinary. With this look, she's ready to take on the *extraordinary*. Christy, make the sound of victory you're feeling right now."

Christy raised her eyebrows and shook her head.

"Come now, Christy. You told me you were fully dedicated."

She turned away and wiped her eyes.

Mr. Griffin faced us. "One reason that so few people achieve the extraordinary is that we get embarrassed by the power of our own greatness. Don't let Christy fall into that trap. If you believe in her, let her know."

Jarod, who never minded making an ass of himself in class, pumped his fist and started chanting, "Christy! Christy!"

Darnell and I looked at each other. I shrugged and joined in. Darnell threw his fist in the air. Ordinarily, teachers quieted us down when we started getting too rowdy, but Mr. Griffin screamed, "Louder!"

"Christy! Christy!"

"Don't let her stand there alone. If you believe in her, get on your feet."

Jarod was the first to rise. This math class was finally jiving with him. Once he was up, Darnell and I also stood up. "Christy! Christy!"

"You see, Christy," Mr. Griffin said, "you can't embarrass yourself in front of them. They're all behind you. They all believe in you. Now, let me hear the sound of victory."

Christy thrust her arms high, "Yeah!"

"Do it again. Louder"

"Yeaaaaaaaah!"

"Once again, but this time, I want everyone who believes in Christy to join in. Go!"

We all shouted. Jarod took her in a bear hug. When he let go, Darnell stepped forward, with arms halfway out, then backed off, hovering just beyond her reach.

"Now stop," Mr. Griffin said.

The class grew quiet.

"Everyone take your seats. That was the easy part."

Easy?

"Tell me, Christy, what would you do to make that vision a reality?"

"Anything."

"Anything? Be careful what you commit to. To get you there, we may have to put that 'anything' to the test."

Christy nodded. "What do I do now?"

"First, take a notecard. You're going to create what I call an Outcome Card." Mr. Griffin handed her one from his desk. "Write on the top:

I intend to captain the girls' swim team to Victory in the State Championship on . . .

"When's the championship?"

"March 8th."

I intend to captain the girls' swim team to victory in the State Championships on March 8th. To accomplish this, I will do the following:

"Got it," Christy looked up. "What do I write next?"

"I have no idea," Mr. Griffin said.

"That's all that goes on the card?"

"No. You need to write down the steps you'll take."

"What are the steps?" Christy asked.

"How should I know?" Mr. Griffin shrugged. "I don't know what it takes to win at swimming. I can't even do the backstroke."

"You don't know? So we've done all of this for nothing?"

"Hardly for nothing. Tell me what you need to do."

Christy slumped in her chair. "I don't know."

"I think you know far more than you're letting on. And if you're truly stuck, I bet you can find others willing to lend you a hand."

Turning to the class, he said, "Raise your hand if you're willing to help Christy find the answers she needs."

All of us raised our hands.

Turning back to Christy, he said, "I'll help too. Just don't expect others to have the answers for you. You'll get plenty of suggestions, probably more than you can handle, but the ultimate decision has to rest with you. Understand?"

Christy nodded.

"Now, tell me one thing you need to do to captain your team to the Championship."

Christy bit the end of her pen. "Get a decent coach I guess."

"I'm not sure a decent coach will cut it at this point, are you?"

Christy sat straighter. "No. To save us, we need an amazing coach."

"Excellent, so now add to your card:

1. Find an amazing coach

Christy wrote it down. "But how do I do that? We don't even have the budget to hire one."

"True. Since this is such an important step, and since it will have a distinct timeline and its own collection of steps, I think it merits a notecard of its own." Mr. Griffin handed her another card. "This time, write at the top:

I intend to find an amazing coach for the girls swim team by . . .

"When do you need the coach by?" Mr. Griffin asked.

"We need her already."

"How long can you give it?"

Christy thought for a moment. "I'd say no more than two weeks."

"Then write:

I intend to find an amazing coach for the girls' swim team by November 24. To accomplish this, I will do the following steps.

"Now we're back where we started," Christy said. "I don't know what to put down."

"As you were brave enough to go first, I'm going to help you with this card. You yourself said that a good coach just won't cut it. You need an amazing coach. Tell me, who are the best swimming coaches in the world?"

"I don't know. I suppose the Olympics coaches. Or the coaches of the top college programs."

"Excellent. Start with them."

Christy shot up in her chair. "I can't do that!"

"Why not?"

"What do you want me to do, call the Russian Olympics coach and tell her I'm a high school student looking for a swim coach, and oh yeah, I have no budget to pay you, but would you help me out by coaching me for free?"

"I'd be inclined to start with the US Olympics coach rather than the Russian, but why not? Worst case, you'll get a no, which leaves you no worse off than you are now."

"I'm guaranteed to get a no, so why bother wasting my time?"

"Granted, if you call her up and yap like a whiny teenager, 'I'm looking for a coach who's willing to work for free,' then you'll get a no."

"So what do I say?"

"Don't tell her what you want her to do, tell her why you want her to do it."

Christy brow pinched. "I want her to do it because we need a coach."

"No, that's still what you *want her to do*." Mr. Griffin groaned. "You need to sell her on your vision."

Christy tilted her head. "How do I do that?"

"Tell me, why do you need a coach?" Mr. Griffin tapped his pen against his palm.

"So we can win."

"And what will you do if you win?"

"Dedicate the victory to Coach Silver's memory."

"Why?"

"She was an amazing coach and got killed by a drunk driver." Christy pursed her lips. "We miss her."

"That" Mr. Griffin pointed his pen at her, "is a lot more compelling than 'we want a coach for free.'"

"Yeah," Jarod said, "when you first said you wanted a new coach, I didn't care all that much. But when you stood in front of the class and dreamed up your win at State's, I got all excited for you."

Christy turned to face him. "Really?"

"For sure."

"So," Mr. Griffin said, "now can you think of what you could say to a top coach?"

"I guess I could tell her about Coach Silver and how she was killed and how we want to win State's and dedicate the win in her memory."

Jarod added, "Even I'd coach your team if you talked to me like that."

Christy smacked him on the side of the head. "You can barely even float."

"You have a powerful vision, Christy," Mr. Griffin said. "It's my experience that the best coaches love their sport and love helping others improve. Throw in a good cause, and I think you'll be surprised at how willing they'll be to help."

"That doesn't mean she'd move here from Russia to coach us," Christy said.

"Still on the Russian Olympics coach?" Mr. Griffin asked. "No, she won't move here to work with you. But you've defined success too narrowly. If you're looking for one of these coaches to quit their job and coach you instead, you're dreaming."

"But I need a coach." Christy turned her hands up. "How else could I define success?"

"Class, any of you have any thoughts?"

"I think," Darnell said, "that you could ask them if there's any help they'd be willing to give, even if it's not actually coaching you. Maybe they could give you tips or something."

"We need more than just advice at this point."

"Of course you do," Mr. Griffin said, "but Darnell's right. You don't need to get everything on the first call. The Russian Olympics coach is connected to top coaches all over the world, including some who live several thousand miles closer. She might be willing to make an introduction or even look at a video of one of your practices and give you feedback over video conference."

"You really think she'd say yes?"

"Absolutely," Mr. Griffin said. "I think there's at least a 10% chance."

Whatever light had built up in Christy's eyes went out. "Only 10%? So now we're back to nowhere."

"Not even close. Tell me, what separates great salespeople from ordinary ones?"

Christy shrugged. "I suppose it's the ability to get people to say yes."

"That's the second greatest distinction. More important is the ability to hear the word no."

"How does that help?" Jarod asked.

"Ordinary salespeople go out on a sales call, and if they get a no, they get discouraged. The great ones hear no after no and keep going. Some even tell themselves that they need to hear no ten times to get one yes. Getting a no actually excites them, as they tell themselves that it brings them closer and closer to getting a yes."

"What are you saying?" Christy asked.

"Like I told you before, each time you reach a world class coach and tell her your story, you might have a 10% chance of getting her to help you out. So if you're only willing to call one or two coaches, the odds are that you'll fail. But remember, this is a math class. What would happen to your odds if you called 20?"

"Now you want me to call 20 of the best coaches in the world?"

"A few minutes ago, when I asked you what you'd be willing to do to reach your goal, you said *anything*. Now you're telling me that making 20 phone calls is beyond you?"

"I guess not."

"Good. So on your second notecard, write down the following steps:

1. Research the top swimming coaches in the world
2. Make a list of 20 World Class Coaches to reach out to

"But here's the thing, if you call with the expectation of getting a no, they'll detect that in your voice. Before each call, you must reconnect with your vision and fully believe that you'll get a yes."

"That makes sense to me," Christy said. "Coach Silver always told us that no matter how strong our competition, we could never go into a race thinking we were going to lose."

"Excellent, then add to your card:

3. Before each call, I will reconnect with my vision and get myself into a peak state

"Peak state?"

"Yes, in an excited, high energy, positive state of being. When you're in a peak state, it's contagious. Let's add one more:

---

4.   Call each coach, and be open to whatever help they offer to give

---

"Are you willing to do all of that?"

"Yes, Mr. Griffin."

"If you do all of that, I expect that before your two-week deadline you'll have the coaching you need. Remember to read your cards every morning and night and check off the app each time. Your 30-day commitment starts now."

The bell rang.

"Remember, all of you committed to help Christy. Homework for tonight, I want everyone researching the world's top swimming coaches. Names are good, but let's not settle for good. Go the extra mile and get Christy phone numbers as well."

* * *

The rest of the day, I couldn't get that class out of my mind. At first, Mr. Griffin had seemed like an insensitive jerk. Rather than sympathizing with Christy's situation, he attacked her. I'd done that plenty of times myself, yelling at people when I thought they were doing the wrong thing, and it only resulted in a blowup. I learned that if I wanted people to respond to me, I was better off being sympathetic. Yet, despite his attacks, Christy had shifted, and even I believed that she might be able to find herself a coach now. How had he done that?

As soon as I got home, I created a new Google Sheet entitled *The World's Top Swimming Coaches*. I immediately invited Christy, Jarod, and Darnell and gave them editorial access to the spreadsheet. Then, after a moment, I added Mr. Griffin as well. Why not? He said he'd help.

Getting a list of the top college coaches would be easy. I could download the college rankings from the past few years and look into their programs. Perhaps I'd do that if I had time. For now, I wanted to set my sights a bit higher.

After an hour and a half of work, and plenty of help from Google Translate, I managed to find not only my target's mobile phone number but her home number and email as well. I sat back and admired my work, picturing the expression on Christy's face when she saw the contact information for the Russian Olympics coach.

Get a copy of

The Size of Your Dreams

TheSizeofYourDreams.com

Made in United States
North Haven, CT
30 December 2022

30322912R00118